Wendy Mulford's most recent poetry, *A Handful of Morning, Poems 1993–1997*, appears in *etruscan reader vii* (etruscan books 1997) and in *out of everywhere: linguistically innovative poetry by women in North America and the UK*, edited by Maggie O'Sullivan (Reality Street Editions 1996). She is the author of thirteen collections of poetry and *This Narrow Place: Sylvia Townsend Warner and Valentine Ackland, Life, Letters and Politics* (Pandora Press 1987). Her latest book, co-written with Sara Maitland, is *Virtuous Magic: Meanings in Female Sainthood* (Cassell 1997). Wendy Mulford is the co-founder and managing editor of Reality Street Editions, formed in 1993. She teaches creative writing and communications at the new University of Anglia in Cambridge, and women's studies at Cambridge University. She lives in Suffolk.

Helen Kidd is a poet, editor and reviewer, and her own work is currently featured in *Sleight of Foot* (Reality Street Editions 1996). She lectures in English studies at Oxford Brookes, writes on contemporary women poets and is now writer-in-residence at Wantage MIND centre.

Julia Mishkin lives in New York and Cambridge. She is a poet, scriptwriter and textbook editor. Her poetry has been widely published in magazines, including the *Yale Review*. *Poetry*, *The Nation*, the *Iowa Review*, *Pequod* and the *Paris Review*. She has degrees from Antioch College and the Iowa Writers' Workshop. Her *Cruel Duet* was published in the *Quarterly Review of Literature*. She has also edited a special British edition of *Pequod*.

Sandi Russell is a jazz singer and writer who comes from Harlem, New York City. She has written on, and has done interviews with, a number of African-American writers, as well as contributing to the anthologies *Glancing Fires* and *The Sexual Imagination*. Her book, *Render Me My Song: African-American women Writers from Slavery to the Present* (1990), is the basis for an acclaimed one-woman-show. Her short fiction has appeared in *Daughters of Africa*, edited by Margaret Busby, and *Iron Women*. She has received awards from the Society of Authors and Northern Arts for her work in progress, *Tidewater*. She lives in Durham.

THE VIRAGO BOOK OF
LOVE POETRY

Edited by
Wendy Mulford
with
Helen Kidd
Julia Mishkin
Sandi Russell

A *Virago* Book

Published by Virago Press 1998

First published in Great Britain by Virago Press 1990

This collection and introduction copyright © Wendy Mulford 1990

Acknowledgements on pp. 269–280 constitute an extension of this
copyright page

The moral right of the author has been asserted

A CIP catalogue record for this book
is available from the British Library

ISBN 1 86049 435 8

Printed and bound in Great Britain by Clays Ltd, St Ives plc

Virago
A Division of
Little, Brown and Company (UK)
Brettenham House
Lancaster Place
London WC2E 7EN

Contents

2.   '*In name alone a felicity*'

3. *'This then is love'*

4. *'Love they say never dies'*

Introduction

The best poems leave one silent. But this is an introduction.

The love poem exists uneasily as a crossover between the metaphysical epistle, the confession and the kissogram. Its value as the means of wooing the beloved – cheaper, perhaps, than a bunch of roses, and also more thoughtful – has lowered its status as 'high art'. But some of the finest poetry has been written under the inspiration of love: from Dante to Donne, Sappho to Louise Labé, Rilke to Akhmatova. Poems know no boundaries between sacred and profane love – whether in the impassioned and erotic Song of Solomon, the lyrics of the sixteenth-century Mexican Sor Juana Ines de la Cruz or the love poems of Emily Dickinson. *The Virago Book of Love Poetry* also ignores boundaries, aiming to demonstrate the affinities and continuities between many kinds of love.

Traditionally love poetry has been written by men – although love and religion, along with nature have, equally traditionally, been allowed to be proper subjects for women to write about. Woman as muse, as object of desire, fantasy, veneration, fear and loathing are all characteristic of the genre. As written by men, the love poem contained a high proportion of the Boast, Brag or Exaltation, which was an accepted, indeed respected, function of poetry as a whole in pre-literate times. For an example, look at the work of the twelfth-century Welsh poet, Hywel ab Owain Gwynedd or, in another mode, the war-song of a later, less inspired, Welsh poet – 'the mountain sheep were sweet/ but the valley sheep were fatter/ we therefore deemed it meet/ to carry off the latter' – a poem which was excellent for chanting as a child against one's enemies or opponents. (And incidentally my introduction to the joys of the unintended pun in verse.)

Are love poems by women notably different from those written by men? Women appear not to exploit the love-object as muse, and there is little veneration in these poems. There is, I would say, markedly more rage, and sometimes sheer bad temper. Quite a lot of these poems determinedly and ruthlessly cut their Don Juans down to size. They also celebrate the joys of independence, of celibacy, of women and of sisterhood: 'little bitty man' as the Argentinian poet Alfonsina Storni calls him, does not cut quite such a dashing figure here.

Nevertheless, there are many love poems as such: 'To my dear and loving husband', writes Mistress Anne Bradstreet, a note to be found in the feminist Christine de Pisan as well as in Anne Finch's letters to her dear Daphnis, 'The Crown and Blessing of my life'. Good erotic poems are rare, and are to be found more frequently amongst lesbian poets and poems from the ancient poets of Japan and China than from contemporary Western heterosexuals, though why this should be the case I am not at all clear.

Our selection of love poems is short on what I have called the Brag – with the exception of Gertrude Stein:

> She is that kind of a wife. She can see.
> And a credit to me.
> And a credit to me she is sleepily a credit to me and what do I
> credit her with I credit her with a kiss.'

Stein is perhaps the only woman poet after Sappho to carry on the true, heroic Brag – the Yale edition of her unpublished writings is rich with it. Unfortunately we can only give a very brief example. We have, though, some notable examples of the 'Counter-Brag', Aphra Behn's 'The Disappointment', for example, in which the hero Lysander is condemned 'to the Hell of Impotence', or Dorothy Parker:

> Some men, some men
> Cannot pass a
> Book shop.
> (Lady, make your mind up, and wait your life away.)

We had decided at an early stage that *The Virago Book of Love Poetry* should include poems that ranged across the whole experience of love and that we wanted to stretch the definition of the love poem as far as we could. These poems are not only addresses to the loved one, they are discussions and grumbles, howls of laughter and rage. They are pensive musings over the anomalies and contradictions of the love experience, and the love they encompass includes love for all manner of objects. The poets dramatise, tell stories, make complaints, sing songs, chant, write letters as well as employing traditional sonnet, ballad and lyric forms, although there is a notable absence of the ode form. Possibly its grandiose pedigree is off-putting to Shakespeare's sisters.

In Love, there is always the lover and the beloved; many of these poems explore the relationships between the two. From the dignified complaint of the twelfth century Provençal Comtesse de Dia, through to the taut disgust of the contemporary Yugoslav poet, Jelena Lengold, or the delight in the lover's body of the American poet, Olga Broumas. In other poems, love itself is the subject, without a named 'other', as in Christian McEwan's '2 Wren Street'. Sometimes the love-object is humorous – Marianne Moore's lion, or Janet Sutherland's spider in the crevice behind the toilet door. In some poems there is a reworking of historical or mythical material – Michelene Wandor's 'Courtly Love', or Carole C. Gregory's 'Love Letter'. Sometimes it is the absence of love that is mourned – Medaksé's 'It's No Secret', about the reality of a woman's life without a man in a Greek village. Sometimes the persona of the poem is the watcher who warns, or laments or deprecates the love relationship.

We set out to find poems from all periods of history, as far back as 2300BC, and up to 1989, and from across the world. We decided to draw together love songs or lyrics either addressed to the beloved, or invoking qualities of the beloved; poems of the love that relates to home, to the Divine, children, family, place and other non-erotic subjects; poems that render a satirical, comic or otherwise negative counterpart to the traditional love-poem, and, finally, poems that explore different aspects of love through narrative, dramatic, reflective or analytical modes.

We began to collect material from the different cultural areas we wished to represent: the two older poetries in the English language – from those living in or associated with the British Isles, including Ireland, and, of course, Scotland and Wales, and those living in or associated with the USA. We also wished to be sure of presenting the voice of black women and women of colour writing in English, and lastly, where possible to draw upon poetries of the world in translation.

In our selection we have chosen to emphasise the work of living and lesser-known poets; we wanted to produce a mixture of the familiar and the unknown, of the recognisable and the baffling. The anthology is divided into six sections, for ease of reading. Each section combines poems from different times, languages and cultures, and of different kinds. Since we found the juxtapositions between poetries illuminating, we rejected the idea of any superimposed thematic organisation. Each poem exists not to prove any contention about, or illustrate any particular view of love, but to tell its own story; each section is a small anthology in itself, composed according to a contrapuntal arrangement of mood, mode and subject.

There is an epigraph to each section, chosen from one of the poems.

These are: 'Go home and put my man out', 'In name alone a felicity', 'This then is love', 'Love they say never dies', 'In love I woke alone' and 'Your name on my tongue'. 'This then is Love' is the opening phrase in one of a sequence of love sonnets written to a Trappist monk by Lucy Boston when she was already in her 70s. I originally wanted to call the anthology by this title. The author of several novels, and of many much-loved children's books, frequently based on the twelfth-century moated manor house in which she lived, Lucy Boston, until her death recently at the age of 97, had a passion for roses and gardened indefatigably every day. Her words are resonant for me, because they point to the unpredictable, yet clarifying, nature of love. When I was a child at school in Wales, our teachers would point with long rulers at the letters and words we were supposed to read and understand on the blackboard. The pointers annoyed me. They slowed up the process of reading when I wanted to race ahead. Now, I can see the value of their slow, material intrusions, waylaying my attention, prodding into visible existence the baffling abstraction of the word.

The intention with our sections was to do something similar – to render each poem more visible. We wished to structure, but not to pigeonhole, the very varied material which composes our impression of love poetry written by women.

Here are ballads, sonnets, conversation poems, lyrics of songs, poems that use personae, poems that retail the confessional 'I', poems that explore lack, poems that challenge language, poems that use traditional metres and imagery, poems that are prose, poems that sneer, poems that celebrate, poems that mourn, poems that muse . . . All that they share in common is that they are written by women and that their theme is Love, however surprising, and however they blazon it or quietly sidle up on it.

What do we gain, and what do we lose, by compiling – or as I prefer it, composing – an anthology of love poetry solely by women? There is a great deal of love poetry by women that has never been presented in anthologies selected by men. Out of a total of 339 poems in a recent example, twenty-one poems were by women; *The Book of Erotic Verse* included only five women poets. It remains to be seen whether future anthologies edited by male poets will redress the balance. Most of these anthologies are also heavily weighted towards heterosexual love, and the pathos, the humour, the tragedy and the prowess in love are largely seen from a male viewpoint.

This would not be remarkable given the weight of male authority still imposed upon our culture at all levels, except that the common, male, opinion has so frequently been that women are peculiarly concerned with love. So it might be thought that in our poetry we would have something worth saying about it. As editors, we initially collected something like 3,000 poems about love by women, and were amazed at how much wit, verve, passion and sheer cussed argumentativeness has gone into women's writing on the subject over the centuries. I'm also amazed at how good-tempered and buoyant much of this writing is, despite the anger and 'complaynts' – with one or two notable bad patches. [I think particularly of the later nineteenth century in England and America.]

Are there any losses in an anthology representing the voices of only half the world? Perhaps for some – but many women, and some men, will not be troubled by this partisanship. By the last decade of the twentieth century, books by women increasingly assume an important place on our shelves and are recognised as indispensable artefacts by both women and men in understanding the meanings and processes of our culture, and its continual remaking.

So much has been lost and overlaid in cultural history, that it is only in the periods in which the pursuit of single-sex existence and art has, for a variety of reasons, played a recognised and prominent part in historical records, as with Sappho's circle in the sixth century BC or the Japanese Court love poetry of the twelfth century, or the communities of lesbian-separatist writers in the West today, that we have been able to see writing by women in its proper, communal context. Too often women poets, and women writers, have been seen to be 'swimming against the tide', lone voices struggling to be heard over their circumstances and their gender. We hope this anthology does something to undermine that view.

Most love poetry anthologies tend to be exclusively focused on the theme itself. In *The Virago Book of Love Poetry*, we have wanted to demonstrate a concern for 'making it new' in form, as well as in different attitudes and approaches to the subject of love. Some of the experimental writers we have included – Berssenbrugge, Cole, Mayer, Howe, Hunt, Gray, Kyger, Vicinelli, Riley, Monk, deploy new syntax and a new disposition of metre and language about love as a theme. Play, too, is an important element in this anthology – play in traditional forms as employed by the twentieth century American V.R. Lang, or with the sharp tones of her modernist contemporary, Mina Loy:

Pig Cupid
His rosy snout
Rooting erotic garbagë
'Once upon a time'

For the majority of women, heterosexual love is still one of the main modes of love. Since this is not a programmatic anthology, in the sense that we have not set out to demonstrate any particular theses about love poetry by women, much of it does indeed draw upon love between women and men. But, importantly, love between women is featured as well as love for children, for home, for parents and friends, and indeed, for art, for God, for flowers, for one's country. The diversity, the oddity, and the mystery of love as well as humour, rage, drama, obsession, and hope are to be found here.

We wanted to give as much space as possible to new voices – our youngest poet was born in 1974, and many of the contributors are still in their twenties. For this reason, many poets whose work one or all of us admire, are not presented here. We have also dipped into the poetry of many centuries, partly to underline the continuities and/or contradictions between what women are saying about love today and what they were saying hundreds, sometimes thousands, of years ago, and also simply because we want to see these poems in print.

We have included a range of poems by unknown contemporary poets, as well as by the well-known, such as Sylvia Plath, Stevie Smith and Marianne Moore. While everyone, faced with the task of making a love anthology, would create a different mix, *The Virago Book of Love Poetry* is, so far as we are aware, the first anthology of this kind. That is, the first to to take love at its broadest, from its most unexpected, for example, in the lament from the Buin tribe over the husband that smells, to its loftiest, in, say, the hymn of Ann Griffiths, the sixteenth-century Welsh poet, welcoming the Lord. These poems track Love as both joke and joker, as demon, steadfast passion, illusion, inspiration, cheat and quest.

The problem every anthologist stumbles over, what to do about the longest poems in the language which one dearly loves and wants to include, is one we have approached pragmatically. Some poems exiled themselves by virtue of being more than 100 lines – or over three of our pages – and by the poets' quite proper refusal to be represented by less than the whole poem. (The fine poem 'Such Sweetness' by the French poet, Anne Marie Albiach, was a case in point.) In other cases, 'Crowbar', by Rachel Blau DuPlessis, for example, and 'Poem of the

End' by Marina Tsvetaeva, we have, with permission, made excerpts from, although clearly in so doing we cannot do justice to the original conception of the poem. Others proved impossible to cut, and sadly we could find no space for them.

With regard to the problem of Anon, our approach has again been pragmatic – we allow, on no good grounds except the voice of the poem and the absence of firm contrary evidence, the *Song of Solomon*, Chapter 3, to be authored by a woman; similarly with the anonymous medieval lyrics. We have claimed 'Anon was a woman' as our motto when it suited us. To some readers this will of course be indefensible.

With regard to other decisions and omissions, some poets could not be included because they decline to appear in a single-sex anthology. Laura Riding was the greatest loss to us in this category; her views are well-known. Some, sadly, ruled themselves out because, in their opinion, they do not write love poems. This is particularly disappointing as we had hoped that this anthology might help to 'deconstruct' the love poem as such.

Finally, for some poems we could find no satisfactory translations, some poets we could not reach, or obtain permission for the work we sought, as regrettably, in the case of Langston Hughes' translations of Gabriela Mistral, or, lastly, and most sadly, I could not afford the fees. With the hindsight of experience, we would not again undertake an anthology working within similar financial constraints. We could have found a way round this by using more material from dead poets, but this was not our aim since we wanted to present work by a wide range of living authors. However, I am deeply grateful to all those poets, publishers and agents whose understanding helped to make this anthology viable.

The anthology is, in the editors' and publishers' view, an achievement for feminism, although today post-feminism, the current 'open' label, is claimed for the work of women writers. But the open is, of course, a myth – a necessary and sustaining myth that is reconstituted through the play of language each time the poet departs from the safe shores of the known, from the face of representation. Sadly there is no corresponding real space for the mass of women in our society, gripped as it is by increasingly desperate forms of reactionary closure. Feminism is still a necessary politics.

In our view, we are marked as writers and as editors by the transactions between culture, economics and politics that have shaped women in the West over the past two decades. These things can not be stepped aside from. To put it more simply, you can tell something

about where we come from, our upbringing, education, and experience, by the poems which we have and have not chosen.

Finally, the editors have not tried to be fair or representative in this
anthology. We have chosen *poems* we wanted to see included, not
poets. In this respect in anthology of love poetry differs from any
non-thematic anthology of poetry, where the aim is to present the
work of selected poets.

I would like to thank all those poets and friends who have helped in
advising, recommending or making available work to the editors, and
all those poets, publishers and agents whose forbearance and understanding have made the book possible. I only wish we could have been
in a position to pay more to poets and translators.

For the final 'mix', I alone am responsible: the ingredients were
culled collectively, and then I weighed and balanced and stirred,
leaving to our patient, scrupulous and modest editor, Melanie Silgardo, herself a poet, the worst task, of supervising the final product.
My thanks go to her, but above all, to Helen, to Sandi, and to Julia,
without whom there would be no *Virago Book of Love Poetry*.

Wendy Mulford
1990

1

'Go home and put my man out'

Carole C. Gregory

LOVE LETTER

Dear Samson,
I put your hair
in a jar
by the pear tree
near the well.
I been thinkin'
over what I done
and I still don't think
God gave you
all that strength
for you to kill
my people.

Love – Delilah

Liz Lochhead

TAM LIN'S LADY

'Oh I forbid you maidens a'
who wear gowd in your hair –
to come or go by Carterhaugh
for young Tam Lin is there.'

So you met him in a magic place?
O.K.
But that's a bit airy fairy for me.
I go for the specific – you could, for instance,
say that when he took you for a coffee
before he stuck you on the last bus
there was one of those horrible congealed-on
plastic tomatoes on the table . . . oh don't
ask me
I don't know why everything has to be so sordid these days . . .
I can take *some* sentiment –
tell me how charmed you were
when he wrote both your names and a heart in spilt coffee –

anything except that he carved them on the eldern tree.
But have it your own way.
Picking apart your personal
dream landscape of court and castle and greenwood
isn't really up to me.
So call it magical. A fair country.
Anyway you were warned.

And if, as the story goes nine times out of ten –
he took you by the milkwhite hand & by the grassgreen sleeve
& laid you on the bonnie bank & asked of you no leave,
well, so what?
You're not the first to fall for it,
good green girdle and all –
with your schooltie rolled up in your pocket
trying to look eighteen. I know.
All perfectly forgiveable.
Relax.

What I do think was a little dumb
if you don't mind me saying so
was to swallow that old one about you being
the only one who could save him.

Oh I see – there was this lady
he couldn't get free of.
Seven years and more he said he'd sacrificed himself
and if you didn't help him he'd end up
a fairy for ever! Enslaved.

Or worse still in hell without you.

Well, well.
So he stopped you from wandering in the forest
and picking pennyroyal and foxgloves
and making appointments and borrowing money for the abortion.
He said all would be well
If only you'd trust him just this once
and go through
what he was honest enough to admit in advance
would be hell and highwater for you.

So he told you which relatives to pander to
and which to ignore.
How to snatch him from the Old One
and hold on through thick and thin
through every change that happened.
Oh but it was terrible!
It seemed earlier, you see,
he'd been talking in symbols (like
adder-snake, wild savage bear
brand of bright iron red-hot from the fire)
and as usual the plain unmythical truth was worse.
At any rate you were good and brave, you did
hang on, hang on tight.
And in the end of course
everything turned out conventionally right
with the old witch banished to her corner lamenting,
cursing his soft heart and the fact she couldn't keep him,
and everyone sending out for booze for the wedding.

So we're all supposed to be happy?
But how about you, my fallen fair maiden
now the drama's over, tell me
how goes the glamourie?
After the twelve casks of good claret wine
and the twelve and twelve of muskadine,
tell me
what about you?
How do you think Tam Lin will take
all the changes you go through?

Natalie Barney

IF YOU WANT ME TO
STAY WITH YOU

If you want me to stay with you
Lower your voice,
Pitch it
To the intimate moments
And let us have a large pot
Of hot water with the tea.

Translated by Patrice Titterington

Lesleá Newman

POSSIBLY

to wake and find you sitting up in bed
with your black hair and gold skin
leaning against the white wall
a perfect slant of sunlight slashed
across your chest as if God
were Rembrandt or maybe Ingmar Bergman
but luckily it's too early to go to the movies
and all the museums are closed on Tuesday
anyway I'd rather be here with you
than in New York or possibly Amsterdam
with our eyes and lips and legs and bellies
and the sun as big as a house in the sky
and five minutes left before the world begins

Naomi Long Madgett

BLACK WOMAN

My hair is springy like the forest grasses
That cushion the feet of squirrels—
Crinkled and blown in a south breeze
Like the small leaves of native bushes.

My black eyes are coals burning
Like a low, full, jungle moon
Through the darkness of being.
In a clear pool I see my face,
Know my knowing.

My hands move pianissimo
Over the music of the night:
Gentle birds fluttering through leaves and grasses
They have not always loved,
Nesting, finding home.

Where are my lovers?
Where are my tall, my lovely princes
Dancing in slow grace
Toward knowledge of my beauty?
Where
Are my beautiful
Black men?

Elizabeth Barrett Browning

SONNET 22 (From the Portuguese)

When our two souls stand up erect and strong,
Face to face, silent, drawing nigh and nigher,
Until the lengthening wings break into fire
At either curvèd point, – what bitter wrong
Can the earth do to us, that we should not long
Be here contented? Think. In mounting higher,
The angels would press on us and aspire
To drop some golden orb of perfect song
Into our deep, dear silence. Let us stay
Rather on earth, Belovèd, – where the unfit
Contrarious moods of men recoil away
And isolate pure spirits, and permit
A place to stand and love in for a day,
With darkness and the death-hour rounding it.

H.D. [Hilda Doolittle]

From EURYDICE

1

So you have swept me back,
I who could have walked with the live souls
above the earth,
I who could have slept among the live flowers
at last;

so for your arrogance
and your ruthlessness
I am swept back
where dead lichens drip
dead cinders upon moss of ash;

so for your arrogance
I am broken at last,
I who had lived unconscious,
who was almost forgot;

If you had let me wait
I had grown from listlessness
into peace,
if you had let me rest with the dead,
I had forgot you
and the past.

VII

At least I have the flowers of myself,
and my thoughts, no god
can take that;
I have the fervour of myself for a presence
and my own spirit for light;

and my spirit with its loss
knows this;
though small against the black,
small against the formless rocks,
hell must break before I am lost;

before I am lost,
hell must open like a red rose
for the dead to pass.

Sonja Åkesson

From 'WHAT DOES YOUR COLOR RED LOOK LIKE?'

I know nothing about 'love.'

I could go on asking for any number of pages
about 'love'
any number of pages
about the word 'love'
any number of pages
about any one of all its sounds
smells, tastes
about any single one of all its meanings.

'Love'?

Yes, I have really been thinking

There is a cold draught.
There is a fire.

There is a flush on the poor cheeks
no matter how empty and slack
and wrinkled they may be.

The thighs turn into logs
(how do you experience the concept 'logs'?)
in the indifferent wind.

The lips become wounds
in the dry heat.

Heath.

Pastureland.

Mushrooms unfold
through the loose soil.

The wind grows stronger
more bitter
full of shamed memories.

There is no road
leading away.
(I put one foot in front,
the other follows)

I walk around 'thinking about love'
a woman's 'love', an almost old woman's:
'petrified' 'disheveled' 'acidulous' 'insipid'
(or, on other occasions, towards other objects)
'self-sacrificing' 'admirable'

my own
whose, if not mine?

I certainly 'love' my cigarettes.
The more I run out of them
the greater my 'love' of them.
But I also 'love' the flowers
the yellow ones.

(how do you experience the color yellow?)
and the bluish mauve of butterflies
hovering above them.

Not so much here when they are all around me
as in my imagination.
In my imagination
there is you, too.

In my dreams, there also are 'fathomless' bogs,
church steeples swathed in black crepe
cripples, rats
(surpassing the zoo's)
'indescribable' apparitions
'hypnagogic visions,' I suppose.

It happens that I find them enjoyable.
Do I 'love' them?

In my dreams, there also are eyes (yours)
lips, individual hairs, wrinkles, layers of fat,
intonations, gestures (yours).

It happens that I loathe them.
Do I 'love' you?

No, I don't know about 'love.'

Translated by Anselm Hollo

Buin Tribe

LAMENT FOR A HUSBAND

O my hornbill husband, you have a bad smell,
and when Kaaeko comes and smells you
he will take you to Panirai, and your spirit
    will enter a pig.
He'll make you like a curly-tailed pig,
and at dawn you will cry for food.
You will sing out for yams,
the food of the living.

Translated by Don Laycock

Deborah Randell

BALLYGRAND WIDOW

So, you have gone my erstwhile glad boy,
whose body, I remember, stained my big cream bed,
and didn't we mix the day and the night in our play,
we never got up for a week.

If I must set my alarm again,
and feed the hungry hens in the yard,
and draw the milk from my cow on time,

and skulk my shame down Ballygrand Street,
to get a drink,
it'll not be for you I think,
but my next husband,
a fine cock he shall be.

So, you are no more in this town
my lovely schoolboy, and how the floss
of your chin tickled me.
And you swam your hands all over,
you shouted for joy, the first time.
Ah, my darling!

I wear your mother's spit on my shoes,
the black crow priest has been to beat me.
But you gave me a belly full, the best,
and they shan't take it.
The days are unkind after you, they are empty.
I lie in the sheets, the very same sheets;
you smelled sweeter than meadow hay.
My beautiful boy you have killed me.

Anon [Provençal]

PRETTY I AM, BUT I AM WRETCHED

Pretty I am, but I am wretched,
All on account of my husband, for I neither
    love him nor want him.

And I will tell you why I am so desirous:
—Pretty I am, but I am wretched—
Because I am young, a girl just grown,
—Pretty I am, but I am wretched—
And I ought to have a husband who would make me happy,
And with whom I could play and laugh all the time.
Pretty I am, but I am wretched,
All on account of my husband, for I neither
    love him nor want him.

May God never save me if I love him,
—Pretty I am, but I am wretched—
I do not even want to love him,
—Pretty I am, but I am wretched—
Truly, when I see him I feel so ashamed of him
That I pray to death to come and kill him soon.
Pretty I am, but I am wretched,
All on account of my husband, for I neither
    love him nor want him.

But I have made up my mind to one thing:
—Pretty I am, but I am wretched—
If my lover loves me better than ever,
—Pretty I am, but I am wretched—
There lies the good hope to which I hold!
I weep and sigh because I do not see him.
Pretty I am, but I am wretched,
All on account of my husband, for I neither
    love him nor want him.

And I tell you what I have made up my mind to:
—Pretty I am, but I am wretched—
Since my lover has loved me so long,
—Pretty I am, but I am wretched—
Now I will give him all my love
And the good hope that I love and want so much.
Pretty I am, but I am wretched,
All on account of my husband, for I neither
    love him nor want him.

To this tune I make a pretty dance song
—Pretty I am, but I am wretched—
And pray that people will sing it everywhere
—Pretty I am, but I am wretched—
And that every right-thinking lady will sing it,
About my lover whom I so much love and want.
Pretty I am, but I am wretched,
All on account of my husband, for I neither
    love him nor want him.

Anne Finch, Countess of Winchilsea

A LETTER TO DAFNIS, APRIL 2nd 1685

This to the Crown, and blessing of my life,
The much lov'd husband, of a happy wife.
To him, whose constant passion found the art
To win a stubborn, and ungrateful heart;
And to the World, by tend'rest proof discovers
They err, who say that husbands can't be lovers.
With such return of passion, as is due,
Daphnis I love, Daphnis my thoughts persue,
Daphnis, my hopes, my joys, are bounded all in you:
Ev'n I, for Daphnis, and my promise sake,
What I in women censure, undertake.
But this from love, not vanity, proceeds;
You know who writes; and I who 'tis that reads.
Judge not my passion, by my want of skill,
Many love well, though they express itt ill;
And I your censure cou'd with pleasure bear,
Wou'd you but soon return, and speak itt here.

Naomi Segal

MERCURY

Quick, silver! Climb,
my Mercury! Foot-winged and hat-winged,
you are adorable.

He made a lyre from a turtle's shell
and played as sweet as his big brother,
my little one.

He came with the king, and changed
the old people into loving-trees,
my young one.

He jumped from a mountain-top
into the mouth of an old bull-frog,
where he splashed till his heart did laugh.

Maya Angelou

A ZORRO MAN

Here
in the wombed room
silk purple drapes
flash a light as subtle
as your hands before
love-making

Here
in the covered lens
I catch a
clitoral image of
your general inhabitation
long and like a
late dawn in winter

Here
this clean mirror
traps me unwilling
in a gone time
when I was love
and you were booted and brave
and trembling for me.

Judith Kazantzis

WHAT IDIOTS LOVERS ARE

You meet a man
as tall as a redwood
as sly as a garrulous blue jay
as patient as a riding-horse.
You're scalding, your love's boiling
over – it surely is but
only sometimes. He's the same,
boiling –
same cauldron of
frangipani blossoms and toads

– The distance between the
two idiots narrows
to Achilles' tortoise.   What
a puffing.   And
then it stops – they
look down between their
toes, mingled – and each stands
wobbling on opposite sides.
What immense landscapes, canyons,
chasms, torrents pour between
these ten and ten toes.
Too great – the vertigo
is insufferable, the lovers cling, lean
clasp like a church steeple, harder
and harder the cement, the
tongue and groove, the pebble and dash
– the vane cock dances in every
possible quarter, reconciliations,
rebirths.   The pit underneath splits
the great tower
in the end, how can it not?
                              Helter skelter
you see the redwood heave and totter
the smashed jay feathers, the
horse hoof over ear,
the lot curl so slowly down
as if air could hold fancies
and their lovers up forever,
ball-eyed, clamped, grooved.
Pit-props – that's what
they make.   Idiots of lovers
trying out edifices.

La Comtesse de Dıa

I MUST SING OF THAT

I must sing of that which I would rather not,
so bitter I am towards him who is my love:
for I love him more than anyone;
my kindness and courtesy make no impression on him,
nor my beauty, my virtue or my intelligence;
so I am deceived and betrayed,
as I should be if I were unattractive

One thing consoles me: that I have never wronged you,
my love, by my behaviour towards you;
indeed I love you more than Sequin loved Valensa;
and I am glad that my love is greater than yours,
my love, since you are the more worthy;
you are haughty towards me in your words and your
    demeanour,
yet you are friendly to everybody else.

I am amazed how deceitful you have grown,
my love, towards me, which gives me
good reason to grieve;
it is right that another love should
take you away from me
whatever she may say to attract you
remember how our love began
God forbid
that I should be to blame for our
parting

the great prowess which you have
and your fine reputation worry me,
for I know no woman, near or far,
who would not turn to you, if she
were inclined to love;
but you, my love, are discerning enough
to know who loves you most truly:
and remember the agreement we made.

My reputation and my noble birth should sway you,
and my beauty and above all my
faithful heart;
therefore I send to you where you dwell
this song to be my messenger;
I want to know, my noble love,
why you are so haughty and
disdainful towards me;
I do not know whether it is pride or malice

But most of all I want you to tell him,
messenger,
that excess of pride has been
the downfall of many.

Translated by Stephen Haynes

Valentine Ackland

TEACHING TO SHOOT

When we were first together as lover and beloved
We had nothing to learn; together we improved
On all the world's wide learning, and bettered it, and loved.

Now, you stand on the summer lawn and I am to show you
First how to raise the gun to shoulder, bow head, stare quickly,
and fire.
Then how to struggle with the clumsy bolt, withdraw, return,
and again fire.

As the evening darkens, even this summer evening, and the trees
Bend down under the night-wind and the leaves rush in a flaming fire,
I am to show you how to bend your body, take step lightly—
and I hold your arm
(Thin and sleek, and cool as a willow-wand fresh in my hand),
And in your hand you clasp fervently this dirty lump, this grenade.

This thing you hold as you once held my hand is ready to kill.
We intend it to finish those who would finish us – we who are not ill,
Are not old, are not mad; we who have been young and who still
Have reason to live, knowing that all is not told.

In your hand you hold iron, and iron is too old;
And steel, which breaks and shatters and is cold;
And our hands are together as always, and know well what they hold.

Nuala Ni Dhomnaill

LABYSHEEDY

I'd make a bed for you
in Labasheedy
in the tall grass
under the wrestling trees
where your skin
would be silk
in the darkness
when the moths are coming down.

Skin which glistens
shining over your limbs
like milk being poured
from jugs at dinnertime;
your hair is a herd of goats
moving over rolling hills,
hills that have high cliffs
and two ravines.

And your damp lips
would be as sweet as sugar
at evening and we walking
by the riverside
with honeyed breezes
blowing over the Shannon
and the fuchsias bowing down to you
one by one.

The fuchsias bending low
their solemn heads in obeisance to the beauty
in front of them
I would pick a pair of flowers
as pendant earrings
to adorn you
like a bride in shining clothes.

O I'd make a bed for you
in Labasheedy,
in the twilight hour
with evening falling slow
and what a pleasure it would be
to have our limbs entwine
wrestling
while the moths are coming down.

Anon [Welsh]

STANZAS FOR THE HARP

1

Went to the garden to pick a posy,
Passed the lavender, passed the lily,
Passed the pinks and roses red –
Picked a nettle sting instead.

2

I'll go to the church next Sunday
And beneath the bellrope sit me,
And my eyes will be avoiding
Who is sitting next my darling.

3

Upon a flat stone by the shore
I told my love one word – no more;
Over it now thyme is growing.
And a few sprigs of rosemary blowing.

4

Only earth now, shroud and coffin,
Come betwixt me and my darling;
Oft I've gone a longer journey –
Never felt my heart so heavy.

5

I imagined when I married
Dance and song as much as I wanted.
All I got when I did marry –
A cradle to shake and a lullaby baby.

6

Once on marriage I put good silver,
Now not a farthing would I offer,
But I'd give a lot to anybody
If I could get my feet and hands free.

Translated by Tony Conran

Alfonsina Storni

LITTLE-BITTY MAN

Little bitty man, little bitty man,
let your canary loose that wants to fly away.
I'm that canary, little bitty man,
let me go free.

I was in your cage, little bitty man,
little bitty man who gives me a cage.
I say little bitty because you don't understand me
and never will.

Nor do I understand you, but meanwhile
open up the cage, for I want to be free.
Little bitty man, I loved you half an hour.
Ask no more of me.

Translated by Marion Freeman

Michèle Roberts

MAGNIFICAT

(for Sian, after thirteen years)

oh this man
what a meal he made of me
how he chewed and gobbled and sucked

in the end he spat me all out

you arrived on the dot, in the nick
of time, with your red curls flying
I was about to slip down the sink like grease
I nearly collapsed, I almost
wiped myself out like a stain
I called for you, and you came, you voyaged
fierce as a small archangel with swords and breasts
you declared the birth of a new life
in my kitchen there was an annunciation
and I was still, awed by your hair's glory

you commanded me to sing of my redemption

oh my friend, how
you were mother for me, and how
I could let myself lean on you
comfortable as an old cloth, familiar as enamel saucepans
I was a child again, pyjamaed
in winceyette, my hair plaited, and you
listened, you soothed me like cakes and milk
you listened to me for three days, and I poured
it out, I flowed all over you
like wine, like oil, you touched the place where it hurt
at night we slept together in my big bed
your shoulder eased me towards dreams

when we met, I tell you
it was a birthday party, a funeral
it was a holy communion
between women, a Visitation

it was two old she-goats butting
and nuzzling each other in the smelly fold

Christian McEwen

LOVE POEM: GROWING DOWN

I used to be a big girl
but now I am so small
a single raspberry swallows up my tongue

oh little cobnut
oh little boat with the red sail

Bright as the centre of a field-eye daisy
loud as an insect
stubborn as a thumb
busy as a marmoset
chirpy as a kettle

oh little cobnut
oh little boat with the red sail

When I was a big girl
I used to be so tall
I could eavesdrop conversations with the trees

Stinky as a workshirt
head down like a badger
reticent as black bread
difficult as morning

oh little cobnut
oh little boat with the red sail

When I was a big girl
I didn't mind at all
if the river put its cold arm round my waist

Wise as a geranium
sullen as stone
honest as galoshes
sweet–mouthed as a pear

I used to be a big girl
but now I am so small

oh little cobnut
oh little boat with the red sail

Eavan Boland

SONG

Where in blind files
Bats outsleep the frost
Water slips through stones
Too fast, too fast
For ice; afraid he'd slip
By me I asked him first.

Round as a bracelet
Clasping the wet grass,
An adder drowsed by berries
Which change blood to cess;
Dreading delay's venom
I risked the first kiss.

My skirt in my hand,
Lifting the hem high
I forded the river there;
Drops splashed my thigh.
Ahead of me at last
He turned at my cry:

'Look how the water comes
Boldly to my side;
See the waves attempt
What you have never tried.'
He late that night
Followed the leaping tide.

Selima Hill

THE RAM

He jangles his keys in the rain
and I follow like a lamb.
His house is as smoky as a dive.
We go straight downstairs to his room.

I lie on his bed and watch him
undress. His orange baseball jacket,
all the way from Ontario,
drops to the floor – THE RAMS, in felt,

arched across the hunky back.
He unzips his calf-length
Star-walkers, his damp black Levi's,
and adjusts his loaded modelling-pouch:

he stands before me in his socks–
as white as bridesmaids,
little daisies, driven snow.
John Wayne watches from the wall

beside a shelf-ful of pistols.
Well, he says, *d'you like it?*
All I can think of is Granny,
how she used to shake her head,

when I stood by her bed on Sundays,
so proud in my soap-smelling
special frock, and say *Ah,
Bless your little cotton socks!*

Marsha Prescod

LOVE STORY? (PART 2)

He buy she dem expensive ring,
(he get it frum de pawnshop)
He want to give she *ev'ryting,*
(Dese women damn price gone up!)

He tell her story of his life,
(She really couldn' stop he)
But never menshun chile an wife
(Amnesia take he mem'ry!)

Dey eat in high class restaurant,
He treat she to he best front,
But she know dat ain' all he want,
Return on his inves'ment.

He take her home to penthouse pad,
(a basement hole in Hackney)
He tink a move should make she glad –
She musse crave he body!

But when de *crucial* time did come,
She colder dan Atlantik.
De blassed bitch wouldn gi he none!
He really getting frantic.

He say how he go kill heself,
And cry for she to gi he,
He write out will, an testament,
(He mudder get de money).

So, when de ting ain lay on line,
He start get real ignarent.
'Yu tink yu special? Yu kyan' grine?'
(He talk to she like peasant).

She laugh, an tell he haul he arse,
Dey wusn' going steady.
His wife fren was in her schoolclass,
She know 'bout he already!

He start to squeeze out real big tears,
Rejection now did hurt so.
De H.P. payments go take years,
On car, an suit, an stereo.

But when he sees she min' made up,
De case agains he proven,
He feel best tactik now is shock –
An stick he head in oven.

At six o'clock, fren find him dere,
(Is five to six he start it.
He wait till key in lock soun' clear,
Den stretch out on de carpet!)

'Oy, Errol! Guess whey I jus see?
(His fren used to dramatiks)
'Yu wife an girlfren, in taxi,
An laughing bout yu antics.'

Sappho

I HEAR THAT ANDROMEDA

I hear that Andromeda–

That hayseed in her hay-
seed finery – has put
a torch to your heart

and she without even
the art of lifting her
skirt over her ankles

Translated by Mary Barnard

Alice Milligan

THE HOUSE OF THE APPLE-TREES

I was summoned. I am here
With those in all the world to her most dear;
I had no welcome from Her when I came—
No blithe voice from the threshold called my name,
No quick hand drew me in from the rain and wind,
And shut the door behind,
And led me to the warmth of the leaping fire,
Whilst gay eyes sparkled keenly with desire
To hear me tell all 'strange adventures' o'er,
Met since we talked before.

This was Her way of welcome still to me,
Such was our gladness who can never be
So merry any more.
But here is strangest quietness instead;
Low voices – hushed about the lately dead,
Through the long night of waiting where she died,
Whilst the woods roar outside,
And always, always on the window-pane,
Is heard the incessant clamour of the rain
Until the dawn. At dawn
Comes sudden stillness, and I walk upon
The hill-side sloping to the water edge;
And o'er the Abbey of my solemn dreaming
See light of sunrise beaming,
But see no green upon the hawthorn hedge;
The apple-trees upon her garden lawn
Stand gaunt and bare-branched in the shine of dawn,
I know they will be beautiful in May,
But – She has gone away.

Anon [Welsh]

THE SHIRT OF A LAD

As I did the washing one day
Under the bridge at Aberteifi,
And a golden stick to drub it,
And my sweetheart's shirt beneath it –
A knight came by upon a charger,
Proud and swift and broad of shoulder,
And he asked if I would sell
The shirt of the lad that I loved well.

No, I said, I will not trade –
Not if a hundred pounds were paid;
Not if two hillsides I could keep
Full with wethers and white sheep;
Not if two fields full of oxen
Under yoke were in the bargain;
Not if the herbs of all Llanddewi,
Trodden and pressed, were offered to me –
Not for the likes of that, I'd sell
The shirt of the lad that I love well.

Translated by Tony Conran

Alison Fell

SUPPER

There is the curdling sky
and the green spry beans
finger-long and knuckled
and the bird's flat fleeting path
across my window
and still
you will not come

Melanie Silgardo

THE LENGTH OF AN ARM

It is so difficult to love the dead people.
From bone to ash to air.
Never to be there
to see the last furtive looks,
the longing for life, the love,
the books, the trees.

The last thoughts muddle and clear.
The heart, the dying fist,
has just enough strength
for the last fight.

The length of an arm is history.

Lucy Boston

FAREWELL TO A TRAPPIST

This then is love – deep joy that you should be.
Though the world's Gadarene ways astound
I see you and my heart has found
A reason for mankind and an apology.
How slight a chance brings on our destiny!
If death had come when it was due
I should have died as one who never knew,
Without this great content to go with me.
Immured, you may the Unhorizoned view.
In lifelong, solitary thought
Your willing heart out of itself will wreak
The poet's heaven that you seek,
While I, an outer satellite caught,
Dear love, see only you.

Sor Juana Ines de la Cruz

From A SATIRICAL ROMANCE

Critics: in your sight
no woman can win:
keep you out, and she's too tight;
she's too loose if you get in.

Translated by Judith Thurman

Marina Tsvetaeva

YOU LOVED ME

You loved me. And your lies had their own probity.
    There was a truth in every falsehood.
Your love went far beyond any possible
    boundary   as no one else's could.

Your love seemed to last even longer
    than time itself. Now you wave your hand –
and suddenly your   love for me is over!
    That is the truth in five words.

Translated by Elaine Feinstein

Jan Montefiore

THE MISTRESS TO HER LOVER

The word I say is not the word I mean.
You listen, speak, explain and analyse –
The air is empty where our speech has been.

Your tongue explores the salty and the clean,
Savouring our complexity of lies;
The word we say is not the word I mean.

Gesture and tone, the spoken and the seen,
The mouth affirming what its smile denies –
The air is empty where our speech has been.

I touch you, and your skin enjoys the keen
Outlines of pleasure which my hands devise.
The word you say is not the word I mean.

My patterns move across your sense's screen,
I watch myself in your possessing eyes;
The air is empty where our speech has been.

What truth I am is nameless and unseen.
The language of my silence signifies
The word I say is not the word I mean.
The air is empty where our speech has been.

Rita Dove

ADOLESCENCE 1

In water-heavy nights behind grandmother's porch
We knelt in the tickling grasses and whispered:
Linda's face hung before us, pale as a pecan,
And it grew wise as she said:
    'A boy's lips are soft,
     As soft as baby's skin.'
The air closed over her words.
A firefly whirred near my ear, and in the distance
I could hear streetlamps ping
Into miniature suns
Against a feathery sky.

Ho Xuan Huong

THE JACKFRUIT

I am like a jackfruit on the tree.
To taste you must plug me quick, while fresh:
the skin rough, the pulp thick, yes,
but oh, I warn you against touching –
the rich juice will gush and stain your hands.

Translated by Nguyen Ngoc Bich

Ono no Komachi

WHEN MY DESIRE

When my desire
grows too fierce
I wear my bedclothes
inside out,
dark as the night's rough husk.

Translated by Izumi Shikibu

Anon [French]

DAWN SONG

On Tuesday I and my lover spent all night in a wood
near Béthune, playing together till it dawned and the
nightingale sang, saying, 'Friend, we must go,' and my
lover answered softly: '*It is not day yet, O my delight with
the sweet body; so help me love! the nightingale is telling us
lies.*'

Then he came close to me and I was not sullen, he kissed
me three times and I gave him more than one, for he
never displeased me. Then we wished that the night
would last a hundred nights and that he need not say
again: '*It is not day yet, O my delight with the sweet body; so
help me love! the nightingale is telling us lies.*'

Translated by Willard R. Trask

Adrienne Greer

CONSTANTLY

At the edge of the sluice she peels and
peels away her clothes; silence and mallards lap
around her ankles.   Her face is a pale thumb-
print on the river.   Faithfulness forces me here,
pockets full of bread I sail by handfuls, chart
her distance by the sound of ducks billing the
water.   Even when night comes down in half-tones,
she knows I am here: the glint of matches struck
against my watch, pages that flutter like birds
from the trees.   And she goes on turning in the
dusky river, her splendid body turning, too
beautiful for making love.   If she comes to my
room, I'll fold back my crisp, dry sheets and
kiss her face 'til it sleeps like the last
light on the water.

Veronica Forrest-Thomson

SONNET

My love, if I write a song for you
To that extent you are gone
For, as everyone says, and I know it's true:
We are all always alone.

Never so separate trying to be two
And the busy old fool is right.
To try and finger myself from you
Distinguishes day from night.

If I say 'I love you' we can't but laugh
Since irony knows what we'll say.
If I try to free myself by my craft
You vary as night from day.

So, accept the wish for the deed my dear.
Words were made to prevent us near.

Emily Brontë

LOVE AND FRIENDSHIP

Love is like the wild rose-briar,
Friendship like the holly-tree –
The holly is dark when the rose-briar blooms
But which will bloom most constantly?

The wild rose-briar is sweet in spring,
Its summer blossoms scent the air;
Yet wait till winter comes again
And who will call the wild-briar fair?

Then scorn the silly rose-wreath now
And deck thee with the holly's sheen,
That when December blights thy brow
He still may leave thy garland green.

Edith Södergran

REVELATION

Your love is darkening my star –
the moon is rising in my life.
My hand is not at home in yours.
Your hand is lust –
my hand is longing.

Translated by David McDuff

Elizabeth Smart

ARE FLOWERS WHORES?

Flowers aren't choosy
Which bee which bug
Come one come all.

Bees and bugs
Aren't choosy either
All entries sweetly natural.

Imagine a flower
Closing its throat
Against a bee it thought a bore.

Who said object
Should excite act
That *that* was moral?

If only the verb
The act acts,
Why call your sister a whore?

Sin and shame!
Abandon the word
Moral. You can *see* it's immoral.

2

'In name alone a felicity'

Emily Dickinson

ALTER! WHEN THE HILLS DO

Alter! When the Hills do –
Falter! When the Sun
Question if His Glory
Be the Perfect One –

Surfeit! When the Daffodil
Doth of the Dew –
Even as Herself – Sir –
I will – of You –

Sappho

'HONESTLY, I WISH I WERE DEAD!'

'Honestly, I wish I were dead!'
Weeping many tears she left me,

Saying this as well:
'Oh, what dreadful things have happened to us,
Sappho! I don't want to leave you!'

I answered her:
'Go with my blessings, and remember me,
for you know how we cherished you.

'But if you have [forgotten], I want
to remind you . . .
of the beautiful things that happened to us:

'Close by my side you put around yourself
[many wreaths] of violets and roses and saffron . . .

'And many woven garlands
made from flowers . . .
around your tender neck,

'And . . . with costly royal
myrrh . . .
you anointed . . .,

'And on a soft bed
 . . . tender . . .
you satisfied your desire . . .

Translated by Jane McIntosh Snyder

Marion Angus

THINK LANG

Lassie, think lang, think lang,
Ere his step comes ower the hill.
Luve gi'es wi' a lauch an' a sang,
An' whiles for nocht bit ill.

Thir's weary time tae rue
In the lea-lang nicht yer lane
The ghaist o' a kiss on yer mou'
An' sough o' win' in the rain.

Lassie, think lang, think lang,
The trees is clappin' their han's,
The burine clatterin' wi'sang
Rins ower the blossomy lan's.

Luve gi'es wi' a lauch an' a sang,
His fit fa's licht on the dew.
Oh, lass, are ye thinkin' lang,
Star een an' honey mou'?

Gloria Fuertes

I THINK TABLE AND I SAY CHAIR

I think table and I say chair,
I buy bread and I lose it,
whatever I learn I forget,
and what this means is I love you.
The harrow says it all
and the huddled beggar,
the fish that flies through the living room,
the bull bellowing in his last corner.
Between Santander and Asturias
a river runs, deer pass,
a herd of saints passes,
a great load passes.
Between my blood and my tears
there is a tiny bridge,
and nothing crosses; what
this means is I love you.

Translated by Philip Levine and Ada Long

Sara Teasdale

AUGUST NIGHT

On a midsummer night, on a night that was eerie with stars,
    In a wood too deep for a single star to look through,
You led down a path whose turnings you knew in the darkness,
    But the scent of the dew-dripping cedars was all that I knew.

I drank of the darkness, I was fed with the honey of fragrance,
    I was glad of my life, the drawing of breath was sweet;
I heard your voice, you said, 'Look down, see the glow-worm!'
    It was there before me, a small star white at my feet.

We watched while it brightened as though it were breathed on and
                                                            burning,
    this tiny creature moving over earth's floor . . .
'L'amor che move il sole e l'altre stelle,'
    You said, and no more.

Alejandra Pizarnik

SIGNS

Everything makes love with silence.

They promised me a silence
like fire, a house of silence.

Suddenly the temple is a circus
the light a drum.

Translated by Susan Bassnett

Anne Bradstreet

TO MY DEAR AND LOVING HUSBAND

If ever two were one, then surely we.
If ever man were loved by wife, then thee;
If ever wife was happy in a man,
Compare with me, ye women, if you can.
I prize thy love more than whole mines of gold
Or all the riches that the East doth hold.
My love is such that rivers cannot quench,
Nor ought but love from thee, give recompense.
Thy love is such I can no way repay,
The heavens reward thee manifold, I pray.
Then while we live, in love let's so persevere
That when we live no more, we may live ever.

Rita Anyiam St John

FOR ME FROM YOU

For days and days
your words have poured and poured
words heard before
words read before
            of
how much love
how much care
how much sacrifice
so much how much
how much so much
that in my mind
i go to a market stall
and i ask how much
how much are you selling
how much am i buying.

After nights and nights
more of your words come
come proposing
come disposing
wine carrying* in three months
a son for you in nine
teaching job with midday break
a party for you and your friends.

In this dark room
without the shine of the moon without
your words come muscled, come rushing
a nice big kitchen   for me from you
a little car for me   from you

*Wine carrying is a major part of marriage rites in
many parts of Nigeria. 'Wine' includes assorted
drinks which are presented by the suitor to indicate
his intention and finally to celebrate the marriage.
The bride indicates her acceptance by searching for
the bridegroom in the crowd and offering him wine
on her knees.

a trunk box of wrappers   for me from you
a fat allowance   for me from you
ALL you say, EVERYTHING you say
    FOR ME FROM YOU
i go again to the market
where everything abounds
where everything is sold
where all can be bought.

there i see all markets i have been to
the Yoruba woman said 'KOGBA'*
the Hausa woman said 'ALA BARKA'*
the Igbo woman said 'MBAA O'*
so i see that some sell and others don't

And in this moonless room
i see what i am buying for me from you

and i see my tomorrow tonight
and i see the sister of my tomorrow
and i see the sister of the sister
of my tomorrow
days endless and uncountable
if i buy
my place for me from you.

*Yoruba, Hausa and Igbo words indicating refusal to sell.

Maria Banuş

THE WEDDING

In the bridal suite there was a black, cosmic cold.

Get undressed, I told him – to warm me.

First he unscrewed his head,
with the grinding of Saturn,
when it wants to escape the grip of the ring
or like a glass stopper,
which grates against the neck of a bottle.

He unscrewed his right arm,
like a pin from a grenade.
He unscrewed his left arm
like a slender metallic rocket.
He unscrewed his artificial limb from his right leg,
swearing like a mechanic at a broken-down engine,
he unscrewed his artificial limb from his left leg,
and iron groaned upon iron,
as it does in a boiler room.

I crawled near his heart,
put my head on his chest,
listened to his heart-beat.

It wasn't grinding, or clanging, or exploding,
it was throbbing –

Blades of grass grew, unexpectedly,
the face of a hare appeared from hazel branches,
a milky strip of cloud – and a sky.
Then, finally, we cried.

Translated by Brenda Walker and Andrea Deletant

Forūgh Farrokhzād

COUPLE

Night falls
and after night, darkness
and after darkness
eyes
hands
and breathing, breathing, breathing . . .
and the sound of water
dripping from the faucet drop by drop by drop

*   *

Then two red glows
of two lit cigarettes
tick-tock of the clock
and two hearts
and two solitudes

Translated by Hasan Javadi and Susan Sallée

Denise Riley

AFFECTIONS MUST NOT

This is an old fiction of reliability

is a weather presence, is a righteousness
is arms in cotton

this is what stands up in kitchens
is a true storm shelter
& is taken straight out of colonial history, master & slave

arms that I will not love folded nor admire for their 'strength'
linen that I will not love folded but will see flop open
tables that will rise heavily in the new wind & lift away,
                              bearing their precious burdens

of mothers who never were, nor white nor black
mothers who were always a set of equipment & a fragile balance
mothers who looked over a gulf through the cloud of an act &
                              at times speechlessly saw it

inside a designation there are people permanently startled to
                              bear it, the not-me against sociology
inside the kitchens there is realising of tightropes
milk, if I do not continue to love you as deeply and truly as
                              you want and need
that is us in the mythical streets again

support, support.

the houses are murmuring with many small pockets of emo
on which spongy ground adults' lives are being erected & p
                                                    for daily
while their feet and their children's feet are tangled around
                                    like those of fen larks
in the fine steely wires which run to & fro between love &
                    economics

affections must not support the rent

I.   neglect.   the.   house

Sor Juana Ines de la Cruz

From A SATIRICAL ROMANCE

I can't hold you and I can't leave you,
and sorting the reasons to leave you or hold you,
I find an intangible one to love you,
and many tangible ones to forgo you.

As you won't change, nor let me forgo you,
I shall give my heart a defence against you,
so that half shall always be armed to abhor you,
though the other half be ready to adore you

Translated by Judith Thurman

Eleni Fourtouni

IN A DREAM

You were standing in the garden
your garden
no, you were not putting seeds in the soft earth
no, you were not pruning the vines
no, you were not taking in the smells and the visions
wearing black, you stood against the gray wall
the monstrous bird beside you
man-sized
shrouding you in his wings
a bridegroom

Translated by the poet

Jessie Redmon Fauset

LOLOTTE, WHO ATTIRES MY HAIR

Lolotte, who attires my hair,
Lost her lover. Lolotte weeps;
Trails her hand before her eyes;
Hangs her head and mopes and sighs,
Mutters of the pangs of hell.
Fills the circumambient air
With her plaints and her despair.
Looks at me:
'May you never know, Mam'selle
Love's harsh cruelty.'

May Swenson

LITTLE LION FACE

Little lion face
I stooped to pick
among the mass of thick
succulent blooms, the twice

streaked flanges of your silk
sunwheel relaxed in wide
dilation, I brought inside
placed in a vase. Milk

of your shaggy stem
sticky on my fingers, and
your barbs hooked to my hand,
sudden stings from them

were sweet. Now I'm bold
to touch your swollen neck,
put careful lips to slick
petals, snuff up gold

pollen in your navel cup.
Still fresh before night
I leave you, dawn's appetite
to renew our glide and suck.

An hour ahead of sun
I come to find you. You're
twisted shut as a burr,
neck drooped unconscious,

an inert, limp bundle,
a furled cocoon, your
sun-streaked aureole
eclipsed and dun.

Strange feral flower asleep
with flame-ruff wilted,
all magic halted,
a drink I pour, steep

in the glass for your
undulant stem to suck.
Oh, lift your young neck,
open and expand to your

lover, hot light.
Gold corona, widen to sky.
I hold you lion in my eye
sunup until night.

Katherine Gallagher

FIRSTBORN

For years I dreamt you
my lost child, a face unpromised.
I gathered you in, gambling,
making maps over your head.
You were the beginning of a wish
and when I finally held you,

like some mother-cat I looked you over –
my dozy lone-traveller set down at last.

                    So much for maps,
I tried to etch you in, little stranger
wrapped like a Japanese doll.

You opened your fish-eyes and stared,
slowly your bunched fists
bracing on air.

Kathleen Jamie

JULIAN OF NORWICH

Everything I do I do for you.
Brute. You inform the dark
inside of stones, the winds draughting in

from this world and that to come,
but never touch me.
You took me on

but dart like a rabbit into holes
from the edges of my sense
when I turn, walk, turn.

*

I am the hermit whom you keep
at the garden's end, but I wander.
I am wandering in your acres

where every step, were I
attuned to sense them,
would crush a thousand flowers.

(Hush, that's not the attitude)
I keep prepared a room and no one comes.
(Love is the attitude)

*

Canary that I am, caged and hung
from the eaves of the world
to trill your praise.

He will not come.
Poor bloodless hands, unclasp.
Stiffened, stone–cold knees, bear me up.

(And yet, and yet, I am suspended
in his joy, huge and helpless
as the harvest moon in a summer sky.)

Judy Grahn

From CONFRONTATIONS WITH THE DEVIL IN THE FORM OF LOVE

My name is Judith, meaning
She Who is Praised
I do not want to be called praised
I want to be called The Power of Love.

If Love means protect then whenever I do not
defend you
I cannot call my name Love.
if Love means rebirth then when I see us
dead on our feet
I cannot call my name Love.
if Love means provide & I cannot
provide for you
why would you call my name Love?

do not mistake my breasts
for mounds of potatoes
or my belly for a great roast duck.
do not take my lips for a streak of luck
nor my neck for an appletree,
do not believe my eyes are a warm swarm of bees;
do not get Love mixed up with me.

Don't misunderstand my hands
for a church with a steeple,
open the fingers & out come the people;
nor take my feet to be acres of solid brown earth,
or anything else of infinite worth
to you, my brawny turtledove;
do not get me mixed up with Love.

not until we have ground we call our own
to stand on
& weapons of our own in hand
& some kind of friends around us
will anyone ever call our name Love,
& then when we do we will all call ourselves
grand, muscley names:
the Protection of Love;
the Provision of Love & the
Power of Love.
until then, my sweethearts,
let us speak simply of
romance, which is so much
easier and so much less
than any of us deserve.

Diane Ward

PASSION

with a glossy rage
you came to my rescue

a slightly duller underside
in the tender mania which grows

depending on situations, intoxication
germinated indoors its long tassels

reach close to the ground
on which warmth is defined

a transport, an elongated heart shape
whose beloved, thank you, isn't me

who embraces fervor one at a time
can watch and watch the watching

at the base, the round spot forms
a necklace, the central zone

and you, and in your warmth, and massed
together in your shape, not obsession

because that's now a perfume
but yes, the loved one, tugging kind

'and so excessive was the sweetness
caused me' single or double according

to situation   mathematically speaking,
rapture, the pyramid, the pyramid-

shaped, plane geometry and all
the points between A and B

Jelena Lengold

PASSION

He confessed to me that at night he shuts the cat in the lift.
Her screams, crazed, frenzied
hammerings on the wall, and most of all her wild miaowing
remind him, he said, of me.
All through each long night his sweet little blonde wife
lies asleep beside him.
He listens: the cat in the lift, already out of her mind,
butting the glass with her head,
a wild beast clawing her flesh apart,
the jungle screaming down her bristling spine,
rams the wall, batters it with bones of her tiny paws.
And just as the cat lets out her last piercing wail,
in the dark, secretly, he shudders under the quilt.

In the early dawn, before anyone else is up,
my love drags me along by my dead tail
and chucks me on the rubbish heap.

Translated by Richard Burns

Memphis Minnie

ME AND MY CHAUFFEUR
BLUES

Won't you be my chauffeur
Won't you be my chauffeur
I want someone to drive me
I want someone to drive me
Down town
Baby drives so easy
I can't turn him down

But I don't want him
But I don't want him
To be riding these girls
To be riding these girls
A-round
You know I'm gonna steal me a pistol
Shoot my chauffeur down

Well I must buy him
Well I must buy him
A brand new V-8
A brand new V-8 Ford
And he won't need no passengers
I will be his load

(Yeah, take it away)

Going to let my chauffeur
Going to let my chauffeur
Drive me around the
Drive me around the
World
Then he can be my little boy
Yes I'll treat him good

Elizabeth Bishop

VARICK STREET

At night the factories
struggle awake,
wretched uneasy buildings
veined with pipes
attempt their work.
Trying to breathe,
the elongated nostrils
haired with spikes
give off such stenches, too.
And I shall sell you sell you
sell you of course, my dear, and you'll sell me.

On certain floors
certain wonders.
Pale dirty light,
some captured iceberg
being prevented from melting.
See the mechanical moons,
sick, being made
to wax and wane
at somebody's instigation.
And I shall sell you sell you
sell you of course, my dear, and you'll sell me.

Lights music of love
work on. The presses
print calendars
I suppose; the moons
make medicine
or confectionery. Our bed
shrinks from the soot
and hapless odors
hold us close.
And I shall sell you sell you
sell you of course, my dear, and you'll sell me.

Lady Suo

THAT SPRING NIGHT I SPENT

That spring night I spent
Pillowed on your arm
Never really happened
Except in a dream
Unfortunately I am
Talked about anyway

Translated by Kenneth Rexroth

Aphra Behn

TO THE FAIR CLORINDA

WHO MADE LOVE TO ME,
IMAGIN'D MORE THAN WOMAN.

Fair lovely Maid, or if that Title be
Too weak, too Feminine for Nobler thee,
Permit a Name that more Approaches Truth:
And let me call thee, Lovely Charming Youth.
This last will justifie my soft complaint,
While that may serve to lessen my constraint;
And without Blushes I the Youth persue,
When so much beauteous Woman is in view.

Against thy Charms we struggle but in vain
With thy deluding Form thou giv'st us pain,
While the bright Nymph betrays us to the Swain.
In pity to our Sex sure thou wer't sent,
That we might Love, and yet be Innocent:
For sure no Crime with thee we can commit;
Or if we shou'd – thy Form excuses it.
For who, that gathers fairest Flowers believes
A Snake lies hid beneath the Fragrant Leaves.

Thou beauteous Wonder of a different kind,
Soft *Cloris* with the dear *Alexis* join'd;
When e'er the Manly part of thee, wou'd plead
Thou tempts us with the Image of the Maid,
While we the noblest Passions do extend
The Love to *Hermes, Aphrodite* the Friend.

Denise Levertov

OUR BODIES

Our bodies, still young under
the engraved anxiety of our
faces, and innocently

more expressive than faces:
nipples, navel, and pubic hair
make anyway a

sort of face: or taking
the rounded shadows at
breast, buttock, balls,

the plump of my belly, the
hollow of your
groin, as a constellation,

how it leans from earth to
dawn in a gesture of
play and

wise compassion–
nothing like this
comes to pass
in eyes or wistful
mouths.
          I have

a line or groove I love
runs down
my body from breastbone
to waist. It speaks of
eagerness, of
distance.

          Your long back,
the sand color and
how the bones show, say

what sky after sunset
almost white
over a deep woods to which

rooks are homing, says.

Maxine Kumin

AFTER LOVE

Afterwards, the compromise.
Bodies resume their boundaries.

These legs, for instance, mine.
Your arms take you back in.

Spoons of our fingers, lips
admit their ownership.

The bedding yawns, a door
blows aimlessly ajar

and overhead, a plane
singsongs coming down.

Nothing is changed, except
there was a moment when

the wolf, the mongering wolf
who stands outside the self

lay lightly down, and slept.

Amy Lowell

THE TAXI

When I go away from you
The world beats dead
Like a slackened drum.
I call out for you against the jutted stars
And shout into the ridges of the wind.
Streets coming fast,
One after the other,

Wedge you away from me,
And the lamps of the city prick my eyes
So that I can no longer see your face.
Why should I leave you,
To wound myself upon the sharp edges of the night?

Medaksé

IT'S NO SECRET

Your laundry, like your life, has shrunk
to a small mound in a tiny basin.
And what about your heart? You hide it
but, believe me, everyone can read
and see no man lives inside this house
by glancing at the waving linens on the line.

Every wash has its own biography and reveals
the people in a house, their size,
their taste, even what they love.

And on your balcony the story
flaps and unflaps in the wind,
a story with no man's shirt, pajamas,
or jeans beside the feminine apparel.
A widowed wash snaps in the wind and telegraphs:
No one is cared for here.

Do the wooden pins pinch your nerves
squeezing out, and emphasizing loss.
The wind blows the virginal white
wares and slaps them toward the rails.
Your nightgown limply hung comes to life
as if this were its only chance,
as if the flowers on its hem want
to be dipped again in light.
And your dress, crazed by the gale,
has wound its arm, around and around
the line as if to cling to something
that fate would rob it of,
by dashing it, again, again,
against the wall.

Translated by Diana Der Hovanessian

Elaine Equi

HOPE CHEST

It is shaped
like a dunce cap.
It is a bottle of perfume
at the foot of a cross.
It is a photograph
that hums.
It is early.
It is day.

It is a bed
no one has ever slept in.
It is just a dream.
It is a rosary of lentils.
It is the part you always forget.
It is a woman with an infinite number
of pages.
It is strictly off limits
except when it isn't
that being the hour when you
finally arrive
completely unexpected and gorgeous
as usual.

Alice Dunbar-Nelson

MUSIC

Music! Lilting, soft and languorous,
Crashing, splendid, thunderous,
Blare of trumpets, sob of violins,
Tinkle of lutes and mandolins;
Poetry of harps, rattle of castanets,
Heart-break of cellos, wood-winds in tender frets;
Orchestra, symphony, bird-song, flute;
Coronach of contraltos, shrill strings a-mute.
Sakuntala* sobbing in the forest drear,
Melisande moaning in crescendic fear;
Splendor and tumult of the organs roll,
Heraldic trumpets pierce the inner soul;
Symphonic syncopation that Dvořák wove,
Valkyric crashes when the Norse gods strove;
Salome's triumph in grunt obscene,
Tschaikowsky peering through forest green;
Verdi's high treble of saccharine sound,
Celeste! Miserere! Lost lovers found.
Music! With you, touching my finger-tips!
Music! With you, soul on your parted lips!
Music – is you!

Silvia Dobson

TO THE SPHINX

I am cut down

Love had sprung up,
a field of corn,
and now,

before harvest, before dawn,
in the darkest hour,
with sickle and with sharpest scythe,

I am cut down.

Frances E. W. Harper

A DOUBLE STANDARD

Do you blame me that I loved him?
   If when standing all alone
I cried for bread, a careless world
   Pressed to my lips a stone?

Do you blame me that I loved him,
   That my heart beat glad and free,
When he told me in the sweetest tones
   He loved but only me?

Can you blame me that I did not see,
   Beneath his burning kiss,
The serpent's wiles, nor even less hear
   The deadly adder hiss?

Can you blame me that my heart grew cold,
   That the tempted, tempter turned –
When he was feted and caressed
   And I was coldly spurned?

Would you blame him, when you drew from me
   Your dainty robes aside,
If he with gilded baits should claim
   Your fairest as his bride?

Would you blame the world if it should press
   On him a civic crown;
And see me struggling in the depth,
   Then harshly press me down?

Crime has no sex and yet today
   I wear the brand of shame;
Whilst he amid the gay and proud
   Still bears an honored name.

Can you blame me if I've learned to think
   Your hate of vice a sham,
When you so coldly crushed me down,
   And then excused the man?

Yes, blame me for my downward course,
   But oh! remember well,
Within your homes you press the hand
   That led me down to hell!

I'm glad God's ways are not your ways,
   He does not see as man;
Within His love I know there's room
   For those whom others ban.

I think before His great white throne,
   His theme of spotless light,
That whited sepulchres shall wear
   The hue of endless night.

That I who fell, and he who sinned,
   Shall reap as we have sown;
That each the burden of his loss
   Must bear and bear alone.

No golden weights can turn the scale
  Of justice in His sight;
And what is wrong in woman's life
  In man's cannot be right.

Jean Binta Breeze

LOVE AMIDST THE WAR

love amidst the war
nestles
like where you lay your head
between my breasts

flows river green
between the arid peaks

falls
as crimson petals
on new graves

grows
fresh lilies
from a rotting corpse

love
amidst the war

you and I
caught
in the riot
of our lives

Grace Lake

UNTITLED

is he painting with tips
his fingers clamber back
down from the sky not that he reached
the top but as far as he could stretch
& it was so cool and fluffy on the way to earth

the white silk cloud line cleared his eyes
everything normal was placed in the landscape,
too nervous he was to say, those trees will do nicely
for tea, thankyou. but she kept on thinking
of him, alone, proud and destitute or near enough

and she kept on thinking of people like him.
others who sat by their tables with a cup of tea,
their hands a bit shaky, their gold rings defunct,
their cold stone floors, their icy bedrooms,
their dark parlours stuffed with loss.

then she bit off the top half of one of those poplars
and it didn't even crunch in her mouth when she'd bit it.
it just sort of disappeared like a ball of cotton wool
which no-one in their right mind would swallow,
chiffon shawl to that man & his ilk would bring tears

you never know why that's the fun of keep asking
but when, and others waited a while, when she comes
down to earth, we'll have a few tickets, for her to push in
the, no, no, she doesn't know why they bothered waiting
because they were altogether busy with other things

and really they only told her what she knew in the way of
supply and demand but something involved her thinking
power stations in language, those differences, understanding
different imaginations, not pretending some don't exist in
unfashionably diverse dreams, needing laddered stockings.

Shadab Vajdi

ILLITERATE

I know a man
who reads all inscriptions on ancient stones
and who knows
the grammars of all languages, dead or alive,
but who cannot read
the eyes of a woman
whom he thinks he loves.

Translated by Loftali Khaji

Anon [Cretan]

INVITATION

Mother it's snowing in the mountain
and raining in the valley
and a stranger's coming
past our door. He's wet.
He's covered with snow.
Mother – open up, let him in.
Silly girl, we haven't any bread.
Why do you want the stranger?
Mother, there's bread at the baker's.
Send me to get it. Darling,
we haven't got wine. Why
do you want the stranger?
There's wine at the taverna, Mother.
Send me to get it. My love,
we haven't any blankets
and the night's cold. What
do you want with the stranger?
Mother, my small skirt
will cover us both.

Translated by Ruth Padel

Joy Harjo

NINE BELOW

Across the frozen Bering Sea is the invisible border
of two warring countries. I am loyal to neither,

only to the birds who fly over, laugh at the ridiculous
ways of humans, know wars destroy dreams, divide the

country, inside us. Last night there was a breaking
wave, in the center of a dream war. You were there, but

I couldn't see you. Woke up cold in a hot house. Didn't
sleep but fought the distances I had imagined, and went

back to find you. I called my heart's dogs, gave them
the sound of your blue saxophone to know you by, and let

them smell the shirt you wore when we last made love.
I walked with them south along the white sea, and

crossed to the fiery plane of my dreaming. We circled
the place; you weren't there. I found nothing I could see,

no trace of war, of you, but the dogs barked, rolled
in your smell, ears pricked at what they could hear that

I couldn't. They ran to me, licked the smell of the wet
tracks of your mouth from my neck, my shoulder. They

smelled your come on my fingers, my face. They felt the
quivering nerve of emotion that forced me to live. It

made them nervous, excited. I loosened my mind's rein;
let them find you.

I watched them follow the invisible connection. They
traveled a spiral arc through an Asiatic burst of time.

There were no false boundaries between countries, between
us. They climbed the polar ice, saw it melt.

They flew through the shimmering houses of the gods,
crossed over into your childhood, and then south.

When they arrived in your heart's atmosphere it was
an easy sixty degrees. The war was over, it had never

begun and you were alive and laughing, standing beneath
a fat sun, calling me home.

Cynthia Fuller

FIRE ROSES

Today you grasped
the stars as
they were slipping off
the edge of my horizon
and shook them back
into the sky.

You are
quicksilver
can leave me
slow-footed
wordless.

My skin is alive
with the soft imprint
of your mouth.
How many miracles
can there be?

As I burnt your letters
the pages spread and curled
bloomed
like fire roses.

Nina Solomon

FOG AND THE FIRE-HOSE

I woke up one morning, seasick
with our bed tilting
unevenly into the fog.
I was a tugboat, you a barge.
I grabbed my horn,
you fondled the paddles
and we both took off
in the wrong direction, yelling
'Look, I can swim.'

I caught my own breath,
and called to the west wind.
My webbed feet were stuck in the ice
of some unyielding duck pond.
I cursed the geese and the sun.
This isn't my room, I thought.
I want to check out.
My host was irrefutable
and disturbingly incognito.
You did not turn round
and I was desperate.

Today I walked out of the door
with sweat on my back.
I thought of you as the subways
snaked in and out
of their watered nesting grounds.
I wanted to appear before you; a statue,
and then return to flesh,
     saying:
 I am these two women, open your arms
 and they will kiss your chiseled parts.
 Together we will live, a foursome,
 pressed against one another
 in this narrow bed.

I ask you:
If the river is glass
and I put my fist through it
will you pull me up, muddied,
out of the undercurrent.
Will you know me when I stand
clean, before you;
having turned the fire-hose
toward my own face.

Medbh McGuckian

THE WEAVER-GIRL

I was weaving all year, I was closer than you thought,
Though still a comfortable distance from my sun,
Like the goose that summers in Siberia, and winters on the Ganges.

I was your shadow box, your marriage mirror, an unanchored island
Bumping against the mainland, since your arrow lodged
In my hair, and filled my ears of rice with honey.

On your twice-monthly visits to my Palace of Great Cold
You had built for me from the cinnamon tree. I stole
Your dish of peaches at the Lake of Gems, you lived

In the Palace of the Lonely Park. My tree grew a leaf
Every day for fifteen days, then lost a leaf every day.
They fell like moon-leaves, like drops from a muddy rope.

My seven openings do not need the saliva of a fox
In a narrow jar – the fox foresees its death with seemliness,
Absorbs its brewing pain – I could reclaim the mulberry orchard

From the sea like the sea-girl with her golden key,
By a magpie bridge, the seventh day of the seventh month,
Unless the swords are stirring in their sheaths:

These days the destructive north is seldom worshipped –
In autumn the tiger descends from the west, smoke
From the burning leaves protects my jewel, yet unnamed.

Marina Tsvetaeva

From POEM OF THE END

I catch a movement of his
    lips, but he won't
speak – You don't   love me?
    – Yes, but in torment

drained and driven to death
    (He looks round like an eagle)
– You call this   home? It's
    in the heart. – What *literature*!

For love is flesh, it is a
    flower flooded with blood.
Did you think it was just a
    little chat across a table

a snatched hour and back home again
    the way gentlemen and ladies
play at it? Either love is
    – A shrine?
                                    or else a scar.

A scar   every servant and guest
    can see (and I think silently:
love is a bow-string pulled
    back to the point of breaking).

Love is a bond. That has snapped for
    us   our mouths and lives part
(I begged you not to put a
    spell on me that holy hour

close on mountain heights of
    passion   memory is mist).
Yes, love is a matter of gifts
    thrown in the fire, for nothing

The shell–fish crack of his mouth
   is pale, no chance of a smile:
– Love is a large   bed.
   – Or else an empty gulf.

Now his fingers begin to
   beat, no mountains
move. Love is –
                              Mine: yes
   I understand. And so?

The drum beat of his fingers
   grows (scaffold and square)
– Let's go, he says. For me, let's
   die, would be easier.

Enough cheap stuff   rhymes
   like railway hotel rooms, so:
– love means life   although
   the ancients had a different
name.
   – Well?
                    A scrap
   of handkerchief in a fist
like a fish. Shall we go? How,
   bullet   rail   poison

death anyway, choose: I make no
   plans. A Roman, you
survey the men still alive
   like an eagle:
                         say goodbye.

Translated by Elaine Feinstein

Anna Akhmatova

YOU THOUGHT I WAS THAT TYPE

You thought I was that type:
that you could forget me,
and that I'd plead and weep and throw myself
under the hooves of a bay mare,

or that I'd ask the sorcerers
for some magic potion made from roots
and send you a terrible gift:
my precious perfumed handkerchief.

Damn you! I will not grant
your cursed soul vicarious tears or a single glance.
And I swear to you by the garden of the angels,
I swear by the miracle-working ikon,
and by the fire and smoke of our nights:
I will never come back to you.

Translated by Richard McKane

Joanne Kyger

THESE SEVERAL SELVES . . .

These several selves that move one self around, thousands
jiggling. It is so inappropriate to be unfound, whine
around, hesitant, lock the window again, this body is
dissipated. To accomplish, to learn, with thanks, to one's
past history is brought up close. And for a while, with
late spring's wild radish flower blooming past my window,
the further shore is close, is here. I do not want to say
he is dead yet because he has not yet come back, but my
sadness for the missing comes recognised, is acceptable.
Gone with the last look he questioned me with. Have you
done this to me?
　　　　　　Indeed are they my forces or the forces
I am within. That no children come from me to love. And I
am this space in time, this focus, of articulation, that hears
the bee buzz round and round.

Emily Brontë

LIGHT UP THY HALLS! 'TIS CLOSING DAY

Light up thy halls! 'Tis closing day;
I'm drear and lone and far away –
Cold blows on my breast the northwind's bitter sigh,
And oh, my couch is bleak beneath the rainy sky!

Light up thy halls – and think not of me;
That face is absent now, thou hast hated so to see –
Bright be thine eyes, undimmed their dazzling shine,
For never, never more shall they encounter mine!

The desert moor is dark; there is tempest in the air;
I have breathed my only wish in one last, one burning prayer –
A prayer that would come forth, although it lingered long;
That set on fire my heart, but froze upon my tongue.

And now, it shall be done before the morning rise:
I will not watch the sun ascent in yonder skies.
One task alone remains – thy pictured face to view;
And then I go to prove if God, at least, be true!

Do I not see thee now? Thy black resplendent hair;
Thy glory-beaming brow, and smile, how heavenly fair!
Thine eyes are turned away – those eyes I would not see;
Their dark, their deadly ray, would more than madden me.

There, go, deceiver, go! My hand is streaming wet;
My heart's blood flows to buy the blessing – To forget!
Oh could that lost heart give back, back again to thine,
One tenth part of the pain that clouds my dark decline!

Oh could I see thy lids weighed down in cheerless woe;
Too full to hide their tears, too stern to overflow;
Oh could I know thy soul with equal grief was torn,
This fate might be endured – this anguish might be borne!

How gloomy grows the night! 'Tis Gondal's wind that blows;
I shall not tread again the deep glens where it rose –
I feel it on my face – 'Where, wild blast, dost thou roam?
What do we, wanderer, here, so far away from home?

'I do not need thy breath to cool my death-cold brow;
But go to that far land, where she is shining now;
Tell Her my latest wish, tell Her my dreary doom;
Say that *my* pangs are past, but *Hers* are yet to come.'

Vain words – vain, frenzied thoughts! No ear can hear me call –
Lost in the vacant air my frantic curses fall –
And could she see me now, perchance her lip would smile,
Would smile in careless pride and utter scorn the while!

And yet for all her hate, each parting glance would tell
A stronger passion breathed, burned, in this last farewell.
Unconquered in my soul the Tyrant rules me still;
Life bows to my control, but *Love* I cannot kill!

Robin Morgan

SURVIVAL

We have survived
distance
as charted in the miles
stationed like markers
uniformly stretching from her street to mine;

we have survived
silence
such as may fall on us again, for years,
through which these poems will whisper
(may they serve);

we have survived
the absence or the presence
of men
in each other's lives;

we have survived
not having lain
in the arms of the other's reflection;

we have survived
not sealing off
any
possibilities;

we have survived
the rarity with which we are unable
to finish mutual sentences;

we have survived
her step, sure-footed and well-shod
hiking in the mountains,
while I, dry mouthed with terror and embarrassment,
skidded after her in my ball-bearing sneakers;

we have survived
jails and supermarkets, our shared and apostatic
Jewishness, paychecks, shock absorbers, puppy shit,
busy signals, misplaced keys, pigments
of our imagination,
and all the other threads we trail through any life's fabric;

we have survived
even our interknotted now commitment
to us and other women,
even our love,
and certainly our fear.

And yet, this barrier.
What stands between us
she said once with a quiet laugh
against which I squinted in irrational sunlight;
what really stands between us, she said then,
is being alive.

And that, you can be sure, we will survive.

3

'This then is love'

Marianne Moore

THE LION IN LOVE

To Mademoiselle de Sévigné

Mademoiselle – goddess instead –
In whom the Graces find a school
Although you are more beautiful,
Even if with averted head,
Might you not be entertained
By a tale that is unadorned –
Hearing with no more than a quiver
Of a lion whom Love knew how to conquer.
Love is a curious mastery,
In name alone a felicity.
Better know of than know the thing.
If too personal and thus trespassing,
I'm saying what may seem to you an offense,
A fable could not offend your ear.
This one, assured of your lenience,
Attests its devotion embodied here,
And kneels in sworn obedience.

Before their speech was obstructed,
Lions or such as were attracted
To young girls, sought an alliance.
Why not? since as paragons of puissance,
They were at that time knightly fellows
Of mettle and intelligence
Adorned by manes like haloes.

The point of the preamble follows.
A lion – one in a multitude –
Met in a meadow as he fared,
A shepherdess for whom he cared.
He sought to win her if he could,
Though the father would have preferred
A less ferocious son-in-law.
To consent undoubtedly was hard;
Fear meant that the alternate was barred.

Moreover, refuse and he foresaw
That some fine day the two might explain
Clandestine marriage as the chain
That fettered the lass, bewitched beyond cure,
By fashions conducive to hauteur,
And a fancy that shaggy shoulder fur
Made her willful lover handsomer.
The father with despair choked down,
Said though at heart constrained to frown,
'The child is a dainty one; better wait;
You might let your claw points scratch her
When your heavy forepaws touch her.
You could if not too importunate,
Have your claws clipped. And there in front,
See that your teeth are filed blunt,
Because a kiss might be enjoyed
By you the more, I should think,
If my daughter were not forced to shrink
Because improvidently annoyed.'
The enthralled animal mellowed,
His mind's eye having been shuttered.
Without teeth or claws it followed
That the fortress was shattered.
Dogs were loosed; defenses were gone:
The consequence was slight resistance.

Love, ah Love, when your slipknot's drawn,
We can but say, 'Farewell, good sense.'

Helene Johnson

FUTILITY

It is silly –
This waiting for love
In a parlor,
When love is singing up and down the alley
Without a collar.

Christian McEwen

AND SUNDAY MORNING

All day in a daze of your making
of our making   love making
all day awake   to the sleep   of the ship
of the under-cover lover   the above-board sprawl
all day in the daze   of the laze   of us both
in the puckered nipple   and the salt expanse
all day in the thigh   in the sly eye
of the belly-button   in the curve of your flank
in the laughing moustache of my own pubic hair
all day in the nimbus   the haze
in the cloud of the sound   of the mosquito buzz
of our love

Margaret Walker

LONG JOHN NELSON AND
SWEETIE PIE

Long John Nelson and Sweetie Pie
Lived together on Center Street.
Long John was a mellow fellow
And Sweetie Pie was fat and sweet.

Long John Nelson had been her man
Long before this story began;
Sweetie cooked on the Avenue.
Long John's loving was all he'd do.

When Sweetie Pie came home at night
She brought his grub and fed him well
Then she would fuss and pick a fight
Till he beat her and gave her hell.

She would cuss and scream, call him black
Triflin' man git outa my sight;
Then she would love him half the night
And when he'd leave she'd beg him back.

Till a yellow gal came to town
With coal black hair and bright blue gown
And she took Long John clean away
From Sweetie Pie one awful day.

Sweetie begged him to please come back
But Long John said, 'I'm gone to stay.'
Then Sweetie Pie would moan and cry
And sing the blues both night and day:

'Long John, Baby, if you'll come back
I won't never call you black;
I'll love you long and love you true
And I don't care what else you do.'

But Long John said, 'I'm really through.'
They're still apart this very day.
When Long John got a job to do
Sweetie got sick and wasted away.

Then after she had tried and tried
One day Sweetie just up and died.
Then Long John went and quit his job
And up and left his yellow bride.

Christine de Pisan

A SWEET THING IS MARRIAGE

A sweet thing is marriage
My example proves 'tis so
To anyone whose husband is
As wise and good as he
Whom God made me find.
Praised be He who would save me,
For he has sustained me every single day
Ah, indeed, the sweet man is fond of me . . .

The first night of our marriage
He showed me forthwith how good a man he was
For he did attempt no violence
That might hurt me.
And before time to arise
He kissed me a hundred times, I remember
Without a single villainy
Ah, indeed, the sweet man is fond of me . . .

He spoke these tender words to me:
''Tis God has brought me to you
Tender friend, for your sweet use
Methinks He wished to raise me up.'
He did not cease this reverie
The whole night through
Not once behaving in any other way
Ah, indeed, the sweet man is fond of me.

Translated by Helen R. Lane

Christina Rossetti

ECHO

Come to me in the silence of the night;
    Come in the speaking silence of a dream;
Come with soft rounded cheeks and eyes as bright
    As sunlight on a stream;
        Come back in tears,
O memory, hope and love of finished years.

O dream how sweet, too sweet, too bitter-sweet,
    Whose wakening should have been in Paradise,
Where souls brim-full of love abide and meet;
    Where thirsting longing eyes
        Watch the slow door
That opening, letting in, lets out no more.

Yet come to me in dreams, that I may live
My very life again though cold in death;
Come back to me in dreams, that I may give
Pulse for pulse, breath for breath:
Speak low, lean low,
As long ago, my love, how long ago.

Rosie Orr

MOONPOEM

the moon leans
from her narrow window
concealing her webbed fins
in her veil

she smears her mouth
with pumice
blackens her eye
with ash
drifts a fine powder
across her pitted skin

unnoticed
her prolapsed entrails
float
in the cold starry silence
behind her

idly

she ogles the sun
singing to him
through her burnt mouth

he makes a new orbit
in an astonished blaze
hurtles
to join his bald princess
in her ivory tower

months later
a new glow
in the sky

.   mars

Sappho

SLEEP, DARLING

Sleep, darling

I have a small
daughter called
Cleis, who is

like a golden
flower

I wouldn't
take all Croesus'
kingdom with love
thrown in, for her

Translated by Mary Barnard

Anne Cluysenaar

DARK MOTHERS

Behind thin curtains, sun rising.

Today, because I am half asleep,
her plaster shadow looks at me, tilt
of nose and chin, lips opening,
a living mother come to waken.
And I am a child in cool bedclothes.

All night I've wrestled, too hot, too cold,
with old age coming fast, the brain
humming with tension on stiff shoulders.

Now everything's flowing again,
the skin eases on the blood, bones
stop drying to skeleton, are suddenly
rocks awash with gleaming salt.

Past them and out over waves' curve,
towards where mind listens, the coo-roo-coo
of a pigeon binds me to the wild wood,
the gnarl of hollow trunks still growing,
their pith the film of brain in a skull
misconceived but working. Flushes of thought
wrap in colour the scan's dark void, line
the chalice of bone whose wide eyes
can still see.

In mine, that after-image
of my mother's head is changing
to lines of older heritage, coiled
in uneasy dreams, where blood and bone
spiral from the sperm, spilling molecules
into shapes of change. The sun is young
that saw them beginning. It casts an image
on our drawn blinds – the Dark Mother
of past and future jungles. The tilt
of her brain lifts blind eyes
to guessed horizons.

No straight line
draws us beyond the coming deaths,
humankind's, the earth's, our own,
but – as the human hand illuminates
spirals from leaf through word to nondescript –
the sun could craft a becoming, our branch
arrowed from life-tree to open margin.

Just now, a mere half-century holds me
woven into sun and shade, half dreaming
under open windows. There is a chorus
of shorter lives, buzzing and chirping shadows,
a silent drift of butterflies and leaves
and, seeking entry at the curtain's slit,
ginger mog, my angular black Anubis.

Edna St Vincent Millay

THEME AND VARIATIONS, 2

Heart, do not bruise the breast
That sheltered you so long;
Beat quietly, strange guest.

Or have I done you wrong
To feed you life so fast?
Why, no; digest this food
And thrive. You could outlast
Discomfort if you would.

You do not know for whom
These tears drip through my hands.
You thud in the bright room
Darkly. This pain demands
No action on your part,
Who never saw that face.

These eyes, that let him in,
(Not you, my guiltless heart)
These eyes, let them erase
His image, blot him out
With weeping, and go blind.

Heart, do not stain my skin
With bruises; go about
Your simple function. Mind,
Sleep now; do not intrude;
And do not spy; be kind.

Sweet blindness, now begin.

Meena Alexander

YOUNG SNAIL

A body cupping a body
does not make two
that would be error
too grave to be borne
given your season.

two lives in one body
might be closer to it.

You are tucked and seamed
in my blood,
when I dance in my sleep
firelight in my hair
and all my joints crackling,
I am not other than I am.

You recognize this for a fact
as you toil
growing sturdier by the inch
young snail.

When you touch the air
I shall be your mother,
a disparate body
broken by blood.

Nika Turbina

THE RETURN

Your heels sound on the steps
there is a ring at the door.
And there you stand,
your hair surging behind you,
your arms flung wide open,
as night is torn open.
And I don't believe

in separation,
let's have no more tears.
You look afraid
as you flip through the days you've lived.

The train did not come back
along the track.
You remained
in a house
of unfamiliar corners,
where all the faces are shattered
where there is silence
and also much shouting.
And there your gaze
will be pricked by another person's words.
Nearby a lift will slam shut.
He doesn't need you.
What endless stories!
And at every window
indifferent faces
like the ringing of church bells.

Translated by Elaine Feinstein and Antonina Bouis

Sylva Gaboudikan

COME BACK SAFELY

Even to say good-bye
even if it's the last time
even reluctantly

even to hurt me again
even with the harsh acid
of sarcasm that stings

even with a new kind of pain
even fresh from the embrace
of another. Come back, just come.

Translated by Diana Der Hovanessian

Alice Notley

BEGINNING WITH A STAIN

Beginning with a stain, as the Universe did perhaps
I need to tell you about for myself this stain
A stain of old blood on a bedspread (white)
– how can I set a pace? – I'm
afraid to speak, not of being indiscreet, but of
touching myself too near, too near to
my heart bed – the bedspread
was white & thin
I slept on her bed with my lover
and thus was never
sure whose stain hers or mine? And when I washed it, or
rather, he did, it remained. And then

And then she died unexpectedly, as they say
became away forever
except in the air, and somewhere near
my heart bed – But
the bedspread
became of her ashes a mingled part.
The stain, my stain, or hers, but mine
My love stain is part of her ashes, & I rejoice in that, whether
she & her lover, or I & my lover
were the ones who originally lay there, staining the bed
Our stain has gone with her, you see,
This is the stain that

invents the world, holds it together in color of
color of, color. Color of love.
This is the love they spend in order to be.
And she was quite young & I am much older (her step-mother)
But our stain was the same one
There is no double. And she is endlessly
clear; & good. Surround my heart bed
with my others at night
speak with me of the stain, that is our love, that
invents the world, that is
our purest one. Help me to stain, I say, my words with all us

(I love you I know you are there)
the song of one breath.
Outside where cars & cycles
I'm not afraid to begin again, with & from you.

born in beauty born a loved one, before history
   born before your time
Anyone was born
before the beginning, before an era, or now
Loved by the sky, & loved by your name, the sky (all there is
   space for) drops
closer staining blue your bed – 'I fall & reach the sky,
   humbly die'

born in beauty born a loved one
before history I was one
who loved you for your name
As your name was beginning to be your face, equal to
   herself
at the beginning, before history, when the sky was gold with its
heartfelt abiding, its need of you

in my dream you were a child
you woke up on a white bed near a window
in my dream you were a man
whose body was no longer of any comfort
We kiss your name & take care of it
Born in beauty, before history, I am one who
   loves you

Enheduanna

INANNA AND THE DIVINE ESSENCES

Lady of all the divine attributes, resplendent light,
righteous woman clothed in radiance,
beloved of Heaven and Earth,
temple friend of An,
you of all the great ornaments,
you desire the tiara of the high priestess.
You whose hand holds all essences.

O my lady, guardian of all the great essences,
you have picked them up, hung them on your hand.
You have gathered up the holy essences
and worn them tightly on your breasts.

Adapted by Helen Kidd from the translation
by W. W. Hallo and J. J. A. van Dijk

E.J. Scovell

MARRIAGE AND DEATH

We are not dovetailed but opened to each other
So that our edges blur, and to and fro
A little wind-borne trade plies, filtering over,
Bartering our atoms when fair breezes blow.

Though, not like waters met and inter-running,
Our peoples dwell each under different sky,
Here at high, unsurveyed, dissolving frontiers
We cannot prove: 'This is you, this is I.'

Oh now, in you, no more in myself only
And God, I partly live, and seem to have died,
So given up, entered and entering wholly
(To cross the threshold is to be inside),

And wonder if at last, each through each far dispersed,
We shall die easily who loved this dying first.

Carlyle Reedy

From THE KISS

wine pours. the singer's blood
cut lick
& scar
decided in embracing just one moment
the cry of the nightjar.
time
courses

the mottled sides
cooks to juice the grape, to return soon
to that land even in its imitation
and seek for us the welcome earth.

as we are
caught here
our bodies bare
hung slabs of meat
hooked on root & spiced
mad flowers of the ground
to be nettled,
chined,
in a crack of dark
heart
let us
feast,

that we go
abundant
as the children of thunder
mated with fire
clinging
upward

bitten as the certain
air of august
raises in the meadow
migrations of birds;

that the land
not deny
even a snake so small
it is nothing
rasps of sound
arrive, as the insects
no one noticed for the day, blind,
to make awe in this concord
love awakens,
battening the jerk of wing
take flight.

games call their rule
& forms to ground the glyptic
echoes of our temples
open to rouse
all wild innocence lost
to blast time ire & flash.
the old day ending
panning gold
for a moment
all
we ask

the sky
to wipe
airplanes of fledglings
that they ride the meadow
grey bombed out
past finished
rise spinning
new
beginning
on the wing
eat but sun

& clear
the days
transparencing panes over ranged squares
lines also mathematic
that hill bosom & maggot be not
so dragging
holding the meadow
planar soothe
departures in august
& rain, stroke the distance
make a little smooth

the bed where lie
2 in a clutch
new skins casting light
all vision of pleasure
& flush the royal waters
of these selves to prime
free from the grapple
bursting this
bright field in the morning
moon & sun in a kiss

Jane Cooper

CONVERSATION BY
THE BODY'S LIGHT

Out of my poverty
Out of your poverty
Out of your nakedness
Out of my nakedness
Between the swimmer in the water
And the watcher of the skies
Something is altered

Something is offered
Something is breathed
The body's radiance
Like the points of a constellation
Beckons to insight
Here is my poverty:
A body hoarded
Ridiculous in middle age
Unvoiced, unpracticed

And here is your poverty:
A prodigality
That guts its source
The self picked clean
In its shining houses

Out of my nakedness
Out of your nakedness
Between the swimmer in the skies
And the watcher from the water
Something is reached
For a moment, acknowledged
Lost – or is it shelter?
The still not-believed-in
Heartbeat of the glacier

Emily Grosholz

ON SPADINA AVENUE

Driven by love and curiosity,
I entered the painted shops along Toronto's
Chinatown, and lingered
in one red pharmacy, where every label
was printed in mysterious characters.
Beside myself, not knowing what I stopped for,
I read the scrolling dragons, roots and flowers
intelligible as nature,
and quizzed the apothecary on her products.

Lovesick for my husband. She was puzzled,
for how could I explain
my private fevers to a perfect stranger?
I questioned her obliquely, hit-or-miss:
Lady, what's this button full of powder?
What's this ointment in the scaly tube?
Who are these dry creatures in the basket
and how are they applied?
The deer tails gleamed in fat, uneven rows,
unrolled sea horses darkened on the shelves,
and other customers with clearer motives
stepped in behind my back.

How could I say, his troublesome male beauty
assails me sometimes, watching him at night
next to the closet door
half-dressed, or naked on the bed beside me?

An evening amorousness keeps me awake
for hours brooding, even after love:
how fast in time we are,
how possibly my love could quit this world
and pull down half of heaven when he goes.

The patient Chinese lady has no cure,
and serves her other customers in order.
Across the curled–up, quiet, ocher lizards,
the giant starfish and the ginger root,
she turns to look at me.
We both know I'm not ill with this or that,
but suffer from a permanent condition,
a murmur of the heart, the heart itself
calling me out of dreams
to verify my warm, recurrent husband,
who turns and takes me in his arms again
and sleepily resumes his half of heaven.

Sor Juana Ines de la Cruz

From A SATIRICAL ROMANCE

This evening, my love, even as I spoke vainly
to you, beholding how your gestures strayed,
and how the words I spoke failed to persuade,
so I desired you to see my heart plainly.

And to my aid came Love, who took my part,
and willed what by my will had futile seemed:
that from the torrent where my grief streamed
I might, by drops, distil my streaming heart.

Enough harshness, my love, cease and resist
jealousy, even as to a tyrant's torture;
to shadows, rumour, doubt do not give over;
weigh not your peace against such proof as this:

for even as water could you touch and behold
my heart, as through your hands it flowed.

Translated by Judith Thurman

Dorothy Parker

COMMENT

Oh, life is a glorious cycle of song,
A medley of extemporanea;
And love is a thing that can never go wrong;
And I am Marie of Roumania.

Julia Alvarez

IRONING THEIR CLOTHES

With a hot glide up, then down, his shirts,
I ironed out my father's back, cramped
and worried with work. I stroked the yoke,
and breast pocket, collar and cuffs,
until the rumpled heap relaxed into the shape
of my father's broad chest, the shoulders shrugged off
the world, the collapsed arms spread for a hug.
And if there'd been a face above the buttondown neck,
I would have pressed the forehead out, I would
have made a boy again out of that tired man!

If I clung to her skirt as she sorted the wash
or put out a line, my mother frowned,
a crease down each side of her mouth.
This is no time for love! But here
I could linger over her wrinkled bedjacket,
kiss at the damp puckers of her wrists
with the hot tip. Here I caressed complications
of darts, scallops, ties, pleats which made
her outfits test of the patience of my passion.
Here I could lay my dreaming iron on her lap

The smell of baked cotton rose from the board
and blew with a breeze out the window
to a family wardrobe drying on the clothesline,
all needing a touch of my iron. Here I could tickle

the underarms of my big sister's petticoat
or secretly pat the backside of her pyjamas.
For she too would have warned me not to muss
her fresh blouses, starched jumpers, and smocks,
All that my careful hand had ironed out,
forced to express my excess love on cloth.

Sarah Gorham

MY CAR SLIDES OFF THE ROAD

At first there's a lizard, cradled
between two rocks, then the mesa
massed against a strip of sky.

What protection.   What an embrace
the clay is completing.   My feet shine
from a notch in the floorboard,

and the moon passes as though lifted
into its groove.   I have no choices.
Everything I love is near at hand.

Janet Gray

UNTITLED

Not that miracles are
made in talk. Or
that he is my everyday's quiet need:
    erratic lamplight,
    some frayed wire or visitor:
means abuse of music of the dead –

So it is I sweep
    over the shreds of moonlight & wet sleep
    which is the other sex that I possess.

Kiki Dimoula

TALKING TO MYSELF

It's all over – I told you
and you said
– don't worry about it
let go quietly
learn how to look at the stopped clock
        with self-composure
be sensible
realize it's not winding it needs
admit it – it's your life
        moving that way –
and don't you be fooled by occasional movements of the hands
it's got nothing to do
        with you
come on down
dethrone yourself soberly
you were only taking a chance
        at it
forget about it – smile

you had your say

Translated by Eleni Fourtourni

Blaga Dimitrova

LULLABY FOR MY MOTHER

At night I make her bed
in the folds of old age.
Her skinny hand
pulls mine into the dark.

Before her dreams begin,
from a brain erased of speech,
a small cracked voice calls *mama*
and I become my mother's mother,

and am jolted
as if the earth's axis tilted
and the poles reversed.
Where am I?
I have no time for speculations.

Flustered, I wipe her dry
just as she once taught me.
Mama, she whispers
worried at being naughty.
A draft streams from the window.

Heating pad. Glass. The pills.
I tip the lampshade back.
Mama, don't leave me alone
all by myself in the dark.

She chokes her sobs
as I take her in my arms
so heavy with pain and fear.
She or me? In cold winter
a double cradle breaks.

Please wake me early.
I need an early start.
Is anything left to do?
Which of us left work undone?

Mama, my child, sleep.
'Little baby bunting . . .'

Translated by John Balaban

Rachel Blau DuPlessis
From CROWBAR

Me

As She
or Her?

Or is me He?

Also consider for
whom am I, say, being
these eyes, these breasts?
What pulse beat for the icons

ticking off opaque cuneiform wedgies

whether I speak
about Her
or whether, being her, I can speak –
given the range of 'speaking' in the first place –
at all.

Tuning the recorder,
a wider distance between fipple and body
thins the tone
but brings it into alignment
with more legitimate instruments.

What kinds of conditions of
longing   of hunger   for
whom
do I nock the arrow
for whom
wrists bound by delicate leather thongs
do I face the straw-stuffed target?

When even one telegraphic
phoneme, one-half more syllable
sibillent (s/he) you (little flirt you vixen)
close-pulled feather,

defines language and centers
what   me   they   is

(and silvery circles kiss the waiting shore).

She
is a jewel in this setting she
an emerald in the silver rain
I weep.

Moreover
I would construct
a ring of green hills
cover of wildflowers' fronds
bowing under close roaring
winds

a fountain eagles
fly down to drink
river war mirror window paper

to worship
to hold her
in the center.

For she can cast green
over any strength or disciple
of shadow.

Erica Hunt

DEAR

Dear

A pinhole of light. Spaces between the words widen them leave
rivers on the page I look up. Blurry creases in the lines of trees'
reflection standing horizontal in the water. Birds bellies' reflected
there too smaller and larger as they veer. you, on your stomach
peering into it one hand out as if to touch what's just behind.

I start to dance on the back porch to see shadows ricochet across the planks and railings something flowers umbra do subtly but tree limbs dropping over backyard fence in wind channels do spilling fruit.

Black dog in red bandana moves minimally in backyard all day from shade to shade and resists urge to wag tail at my shadow leaning across.

This is like sending a telegram to heaven 'You don't know what you've missed.'

Or perhaps knowing too well, you have stepped outside for a smoke.

Diana Der Hovanessian

RAIN

Rain undoes the stone
unfastens grass.
Nothing is permanently
attached to bone.
Neither epoxy
nor promises last.

But I keep those inflections
you telephoned to wear
with your frown on rainy days.
There is another you
I have invented from your name
and cemented to my bones forever.

let rain say nothing stays.

Anna Kamiénska

LOVING MY ENEMIES

At last I have some real enemies
and I should start by loving them;
we have even signed a secret pact of difference.

Possibly you might mistake us
for two sides of the same coin,
or two ends of the stick.
Our coats hang in the cloakroom side by side,
we speak the same words
though our languages are quite dissimilar,
conjunctions divide us and do not join.

It is prudent even to love bad weather,
since, after all, it is weather of some sort.
I hunt for a point on the map of being
where two human lights at least can find some rest.

Caught in two feeble beams
they yield to love with slowness.

Lord, you know how hard it is,
and that finally judgement will be passed.
Justice shrinks before the fact
that people are afraid of one another.
If they were magnificent wild beasts
it might be worthwhile dying in their argument's claws
       but
          enemies must be loved to the bitter end
          of our mortal truth.

Translated by Susan Bassnett and Piotr Kuhiwzak

Elaine Feinstein

HOME

Where is that I wonder?
Is it the book-packed house we plan to sell
with the pale green room above the river,
the shelves of icons, agate, Eilat stone
the Kathe Kollwitz and the Samuel Palmer?

Or my huge childhood house
oak-floored, the rugs of Autumn colours, slabs of coal
in an open hearth, high-windowed rooms,
outside, the sunken garden, lavender, herbs
and trees of Victoria plum.

Last night I dreamed of
my dead father, white-faced, papery-skinned
and frailer than he died. I asked him:
– Doesn't all this belong to us? He shook his head,
bewildered. I was disappointed,

but though I woke with salt on my lips then
and a hoarse throat, somewhere between
the ocean and the desert, in an immense
Mexico of the spirit, I remembered
with joy and love my other ties of blood.

Geraldine Monk

STUMP CROSS – The Long Wait

Stone Ruck	a place	tired pinnacle?
Tired People	a person	my grandmother?

I was six perhaps seven
She was bone china eggshell
lying amongst candles and flowers
She was wild cold bryonies
I smiled
She was only beautiful.

Worm Sike Rigg	a place	for dead?
The Dead	a person	my grandmother?

Nakahu-kahu	go to sleep
Nakahu-kahu	go to sleep

Liliane Lijn

OUT THE YOU OF
YESTERDAY

Out the you of yesterday
the leavings of yourself
the you that never was you

Pick up the dice
rattle the numbers
let fly your choice

DO

WISDOM PIERCES
the radiant state
cuts it through and through
sliding and slithering oil–like

penetrating

this is no race of tenderness
no petting game
but the body test

the feel of me and you

WARNING
WARNING
QUIVER NOT
TAKE STASIS

WHERE
FLAME
WAS

look to the core
for a moment
without shakes
to there
where it boils
where it never stops

you are sound
take possession of your vision
take your eyes in hand

make I time same

MINERAL
VORTEX
TRUTH

divine near face space
on the land of receival
the earthing zone
ahead and before

swallow light

swallow it whole and full
and digest knead it through

birth mirror nothing
    delights swarm

and the scientific splinters
the fingers without hand
point to the nova
the bursting ones

SACRED SKY
RAW WOMAN
STEEL MIND

Khosrovidought Koghtnatsi

MORE ASTONISHING

More astonishing to me
than the lyrics made for you,
more amazing than the music
composed for your death,
is the sound of the sobbing
mourning you, Lord Vahan,
chosen of God.
Let me be inspired in that clear part
of my soul to compose songs for you too,
but not songs that mourn;
but joyous, exhorting praises for your work,
blessing you, servant of God.

Although you found your labor
and your ascetic self denial
which is so terrifying to my body's nature,
more rewarding than praises,
let me praise, O blessed Vahan, lover of Christ.

Let those outsiders who build upon vanity
go down in defeat.

Let your soul rest in divine light, O blessed
Vahan, chosen of the tree.

Brave martyr, it was while performing unselfishly
against the nations of the south
that you were fixed forever
as an immortal and blessed ruler of Koght.

Translated by Diana Der Hovanessian

Anne Griffiths

EXPECTING THE LORD

Being myself so corrupted
With the forsaking life I lead,
To be on your holy mountain
Is high privilege indeed;
There the veils are rent, and coverings
Destroyed from that time forth,
And there is your excelling glory
On the transient things of earth.

O to keep at that high drinking
Where the streams of great salvation flow,
Till I'm utterly disthirsted
For the transient things below!
To live, and my Lord always expected!
To be, when he comes, up and awake!
Quick as a flash to open for him!
Enjoy him without stint or break!

Translated by Tony Conran

Hroswitha

IN PRAISE OF VIRGINITY

Look now, bride of God,
what splendour on earth awaits you,
what glories, too, in Heaven –
    Look now, bride of God!

Joyful gifts you'll get,
festive, brilliant with torches.
See there, the bridegroom comes!
    Joyful gifts you'll get.

And you will play new songs,
plucking sweet sounds from strings;
hailing with hymns your wedding day,
    you will play new songs.

No one will thrust away
from the high-throned company of the lamb
you, whom he chose in love –
   no one will thrust away.

Translated by John Dillon

Angelina Grimké

EL BESO

Twilight – and you,
Quiet – the stars;
Snare of the shine of your teeth,
Your provocative laughter,
The gloom of your hair;
Lure of you, eye and lip,
Yearning, yearning,
Languor, surrender;
       Your mouth
And madness, madness
Tremulous, breathless, flaming,
The space of a sigh;
Then awaking – remembrance,
Pain, regret – your sobbing;
And again quiet – the stars,
Twilight – and you.

Muriel Rukeyser

LOOKING AT EACH OTHER

Yes, we were looking at each other
Yes, we knew each other very well
Yes, we had made love with each other many times
Yes, we had heard music together
Yes, we had gone to the sea together
Yes, we had cooked and eaten together
Yes, we had laughed often day and night
Yes, we fought violence and knew violence
Yes, we hated the inner and outer oppression

Yes, that day we were looking at each other
Yes, we saw the sunlight pouring down
Yes, the corner of the table was between us
Yes, bread and flowers were on the table
Yes, our eyes saw each other's eyes
Yes, our mouths saw each other's mouth
Yes, our breasts saw each other's breasts
Yes, our bodies entire saw each other
Yes, it was beginning in each
Yes, it threw waves across our lives
Yes, the pulses were becoming very strong
Yes, the beating became very delicate
Yes, the calling   the arousal
Yes, the arriving   the coming
Yes, there it was for both entire
Yes, we were looking at each other

Anne Stevenson

THE VICTORY

I thought you were my victory
though you cut me like a knife
when I brought you out of my body
into your life.

Tiny antagonist, gory,
blue as a bruise. The stains
of your cloud of glory
bled from my veins.

How can you dare, blind thing,
blank insect eyes?
You barb the air. You sting
with bladed cries.

Snail! Scary knot of desires!
Hungry snarl! Small son.
Why do I have to love you?
How have you won?

Audre Lorde

NOW THAT I AM FOREVER WITH CHILD

How the days went
while you were blooming within me
I remember each upon each —
the swelling changed planes of my body
and how you first fluttered, then jumped
and I thought it was my heart.

How the days wound down
and the turning of winter
I recall with you growing heavy
against the wind. I thought
now her hands
are formed, and her hair
has started to curl
now her teeth are done
now she sneezes.
Then the seed opened
I bore you one morning just before spring
My head rang like a fiery piston
my legs were towers between which
A new world was passing.

Since then
I can only distinguish
one thread within running hours
You, flowing through selves
toward You.

Doina Uricariu

SMALL SPLINTERS FROM MY CHEEK

Happiness blood from my blood.

Sometimes truth keeps quiet
pretending to be something else:
I talk about the claws of a bird,
they scratch into my shoulder,

But this strange tale describes
the time just after feeding,
tender, ferocious, domestic,
hair done up in plaits,
the small body has turned its back
and serenely submerges into me.

Happiness usurps and steals.
Small splinters from my cheek hit me.

Translated by Brenda Walker and Andrea Deletant

Sylvia Plath

ZOO KEEPER'S WIFE

I can stay awake all night, if need be –
Cold as an eel, without eyelids.
Like a dead lake the dark envelops me,
Blueblack, a spectacular plum fruit.
No airbubbles start from my heart, I am lungless
And ugly, my belly a silk stocking
Where the heads and tails of my sisters decompose.
Look, they are melting like coins in the powerful juices –

The spidery jaws, the spine bones bared for a moment
Like the white lines on a blueprint.
Should I stir, I think this pink and purple plastic
Guts bag would clack like a child's rattle,
Old grievances jostling each other, so many loose teeth.
But what do you know about that
My fat pork, my marrowy sweetheart, face-to-the-wall?
Some things of this world are indigestible.

You wooed me with the wolf-headed fruit bats
Hanging from their scorched hooks in the moist
Fug of the Small Mammal House.
The armadillo dozed in his sandbin
Obscene and bald as a pig, the white mice
Multiplied to infinity like angels on a pinhead
Out of sheer boredom. Tangled in the sweat-wet sheets
I remembered the bloodied chicks and the quartered rabbits.

You checked the diet charts and took me to play
With the boa constrictor in the Fellows' Garden.
I pretended I was the Tree of Knowledge.
I entered your bible, I boarded your ark
With the sacred baboon in his wig and wax ears
And the bear-furred, bird-eating spider
Clambering round its glass box like an eight-fingered hand.
I can't get it out of my mind

How our courtship lit the tindery cages –
Your two-horned rhinoceros opened a mouth
Dirty as a bootsole and big as a hospital sink
For my cube of sugar: its bog breath
Gloved my arm to the elbow.
The snails blew kisses like black apples.
Nightly now I flog apes owls bears sheep
Over their iron stile. And still don't sleep.

May Sarton

A LIGHT LEFT ON

In the evening we came back
Into our yellow room,
For a moment taken aback
To find the light left on,
Falling on silent flowers
Table, book, empty chair
While we had gone elsewhere,
Had been away for hours.

When we came home together
We found the inside weather.
All of our love unended
The quiet light demanded,
And we gave, in a look
At yellow walls and open book.
The deepest world we share
And do not talk about
But have to have, was there,
And by that light found out.

U.A. Fanthorpe

HOMING IN

Somewhere overseas England are struggling
On a sticky wicket; somewhere in Europe
An elder statesman is dying *adagio*; and here,
Nowhere precisely, I slip to pips and bens
Through the occupied air.

Somewhere along this road an invisible ditch
Signals tribe's end, an important mutation of [ʌ];
Somewhere among these implacable place-names
People are living coherent lives. For me the unfocussed
Landscape of exile.

Somewhere along this watershed weather
Will assert itself, swap wet for dry,
Scribble or flare on windscreens, send freak gusts
Sneaking round juggernauts, ravel traffic with
A long foggy finger.

Home starts at Birmingham. Places
Where I have walked are my auguries:
The stagey Malverns, watery sharp Bredon,
May Hill's arboreal quiff. These as I pass
Will bring me luck if they look my way.

I should be rehearsing contingencies,
Making resolutions, allowing for change
In the tricky minor modes of love. But,
Absorbed by nearly-home names,
Dear absurd Saul, Framilode, Frampton-on-Severn,

I drop, unprepared, into one particular
Parish, one street, one house, one you,
Exact, ignorant and faithful as swallows commuting
From Sahara to garage shelf.

4

'Love they say never dies'

Sonia Sanchez

FOR OUR LADY

yeh.
    billie.   if someone
had loved u like u
shud have been loved
ain't no tellen what
kinds of songs
          u wud have swung
gainst this country's wite mind.
or what kinds of lyrics
          wud have pushed us from
our blue/nites.
        yeh.   billie.
if some blk/man
        had reallee
made u feel
      permanentlee warm.
ain't no tellen
      where the jazz of yo/songs.
      wud have led us.

Gillian Clarke

From LETTER FROM A FAR COUNTRY

The sea stirs restlessly between
the sweetness of clean sheets,
the lifted arms,
the rustling petticoats.

My mother's laundry list, ready
on Mondays when the van called.
The rest soaked in glutinous starch
and whitened with a bluebag
kept in a broken cup.

(In the airing cupboard you'll see
a map, numbering and placing
every towel, every sheet.
I have charted all your needs.)

It has always been a matter
of lists. We have been counting,
folding, measuring, making,
tenderly laundering cloth
ever since we have been women.

The waves are folded meticulously,
perfectly white. Then they are tumbled
and must come to be folded again.

Four herring gulls and their shadows
are shouting at the clear glass
of a shaken wave. The sea's a sheet
bellying in the wind, snapping.
Air and white linen. Our airing cupboards
are full of our satisfactions.

The gulls grieve at our contentment.
It is a masculine question.
'Where' they call 'are your great works?'
They slip their fetters and fly up
to laugh at land-locked women.
Their cries are cruel as greedy babies.

Our milky tendernesses dry
to crisp lists; immaculate
linen; jars labelled and glossy
with our perfect preserves.
Spiced oranges; green tomato
chutney; seville orange marmalade
annually staining gold
the snows of January

(the saucers of marmalade
are set when the amber wrinkles
like the sea if you blow it)

Jams and jellies of blackberry,
crabapple, strawberry, plum,
greengage and loganberry.
You can see the fruit pressing
their little faces against the glass;
tiny onions imprisoned
in their preservative juices.

Familiar days are stored whole
in bottles. There's a wet morning
orchard in the dandelion wine;
a white spring distilled
in elderflower's clarity;
and a loving, late, sunburning
day of October in syrups
of rose hip and the beautiful
black sloes that stained the gin to rose.

It is easy to make of love
these ceremonials. As priests
we fold cloth, break bread; share wine,
hope there's enough to go round.

(You'll find my inventories pinned
inside all of the cupboard doors.)

Gwendolyn Brooks

BLACK LOVE

Black love, provide the adequate electric
for what is lapsed and lenient in us now.

Rouse us from blur. Call us.

Call adequately the postponed corner brother.
And call our man in the pin-stripe suiting and restore
him to his abler logic; to his people.

Call to the shattered sister and repair her
in her difficult hour, narrow her fever.

Call to the Elders –
our customary grace and further sun
loved in the Long-ago, loathed in the Lately;
a luxury of languish and of rust.

Appraise, assess our Workers in the Wild, lest they
descend to malformation and to undertow.

Black love, define and escort our young, be means and
    redemption, discipline.

Nourish our children – proud, strong
little men upright-easy:
quick
flexed
little stern-warm historywomen . . .
I see them in Ghana, Kenya, in the city of Dar-es-
    Salaam, in Kalamazoo, Mound Bayou, in Chicago.

Lovely loving children
with long soft eyes.

Black love, prepare us all for interruptions;
assaults, unwanted pauses; furnish for leavings and
    for losses.

Just come out Blackly glowing!

On the ledges – in the lattices – against the failing
    light of
candles that stutter,
and in the chop and challenge of our apprehension –
be
the Alwayswonderful of this world.

Joyce Carol Oates

HOW GENTLE

how gentle are we rising
easy as eyes in sockets turning

intimate the hardness: jaw
upon jaw, forehead warm

upon forehead
kisses quick as breaths, without volition

Love: I am luminous
careless as love's breathing

fluorescent glowing the fine
warm veins and bones

your weight,
the sky lowered suddenly

I am loved: a message
clanging of a bell in silence

you are quickened with surprise
our horizons surrender to walls

Are we wearing out
our skins' defenses? –

turning to silk, texture of flashy
airy surfaces scant as breaths?

I am loved: the noon slides gently
suddenly upon us
to wake us

Daphne Marlatt

LONG TIME COMING

Sea hood, snail, born with a caul on his head,
tumbles in weedy medium of now. Semen falls as
dizziness. sink back to head   tail   snail   objects. weeds to catch at his shell like hair,
cilia he put his foot on now grabs hold.   eye
feeling thru rain

                       am not down.   water runs down
the windowpane i face.   disaffections.   might order
a new order as water waves its snail pace . . .

snared in a diver's hold. i come up for breath.
around & over our heads the sound of moss fingers
our eaves.   melt.   snow purple at eyes' level
swallows from view.   two.   in a cell.   i keep coming
up for breath, crackle of light fragments, genes.
help

   'as if there were anything but'

love orders another order of mosses, snows, in all
this iridescent coal.

Frances Horovitz

AN OLD MAN REMEMBERS

*'. . . and Gwdion and Math made for Lleu Llaw Gyffes a wife out of the flowers
of the oak, the broom and the meadowsweet and her name was Blodeuedd. And
when she betrayed her husband with Gronw Bebyr, Lord of Penllyn, for
punishment she was turned into an owl . . .'*
From THE MABINOGION

in this valley she walked
                    I remember
a woman with the smell of wind in her hands
walking at nightfall in the floating dusk
veiled in the petals of an early spring

they say she was made of flowers
flowers yellow and white
                        of spring and summer
and drifted away on wind and water
when the shape spell dissolved

certain she was a flower in our valley
her breasts were flowers red and white
and her eyes and the scent of her
and certain there was never a warm child in her arms

but she lay in her lord's bed and was loved
she bore him his cup and his meat
gold was given her, white linen
and many songs by the firelight
of longing and pride

the valley contained us
a flower for a queen
lust swelled our harp strings
we grew fat on our dream

now I remember
her shadow swims clear
there was blood in the valley
                        a stranger
blood in the bowl and the spring
red sullied white
two lives destroyed
and white petals scattered
in a cold racing wind

some say of that frail woman of flowers
her love turned her to owl's wings
and lonely now in the valley
with foxes and ravens she rules

and certain at nightfall
when the owls cry out
I think I see her clear
a white shape on the hill
– but this is an old man's longing
a shadow, a dream
a memory of harp-song and flowers
and a fair woman walking in the spring

Tess Gallagher

ALL DAY THE LIGHT IS CLEAR

Today I wished without mercy
in the bloodless nations of the mind
that a city had gone down with you
as in a war fought – not
on foreign soil, but here
in the part of the country I can't
do without. Then, if I wept for you
inexplicably, as I have
on street corners, I could say the name
of that city and ignite in the memories
of strangers, a companion
sorrow. 'Yes,' they would say, 'Yes,
we know,' giving again that name
like a fountain
in some dusty village where the women pause,
dash water across their brows,
and pass on.

And though I shame such power and force it
from my mind, you enter this street
as a touch on the shoulder, a stare that
speaks, or in the brief nods
between workers at change of shift.
I lean on their conquering faces.
I add you to the heap, to the beautiful
multitude for whom only singing
and silence may serve – those

of our city, city of the unmiraculous,
undiminished belonging, toward which
in the green fields – as did the women
of Leningrad – I bow, bow again
and make no sound.

Sarah Kirsch

WINTERMUSIK

once a red vixen
with high leaps
I got what I wanted

grey I   am   now grey rain.
I travelled   as far as Greenland
in my heart.

a stone shines on the coast
on it is written no one returns
the stone shortens my life,

the four corners of the world
are full of suffering.   love
is like the breaking of the spine

Translated by Wendy Mulford and Anthony Vivis

Christian McEwen

2 WREN STREET

It was a moment, sudden as snowflakes,
when the shadow swung luxuriously across the wall
and the elderberries trembled on their fine red stalks.
In the house, a woman sighed in satisfaction and relief
at the white tiles in the ordinary bathroom,
no more washing-up. And it astonished me
to live so comfortably behind my eyes.
Thus it was, in the big room with the pictures
and the crowded shelves, a child was lying softly
on a bed. Orgasms came and went like tiny birds.

Molly Peacock

MENTAL FRANCE

We adults make love, but I am far away
in a hut at dusk where two lovers lay
swathed in orange light. Near night. A table
across the room, a purple swath of cloth
on the floor (a girl's dress), on the table
two green oranges . . . blur in my thought. Both
of us almost stop moving in the hiatus
that comes while we wait for each other to focus.

What I used to read is real.
The hut was in a book I read for hours
in school, praying to feel what other people feel.
Now that my desires suit my powers
I find a fresh past in this present, cut
from the literature of love like a fresh
wish clipped from a standard prayer: my hut
in France in this apartment of flesh.

Aphra Behn

SONG

Pan, grant that I may never prove
So great a *Slave* to fall in love,
And to an Unknown *Deity*
Resign my happy Liberty:
I love to see the Amorous *Swains*
    Unto my Scorn their Hearts resign:
With Pride I see the Meads and Plains
    Throng'd all with *Slaves,* and they all mine:
Whilst I the whining Fools despise,
That pay their Homage to my Eyes.

Dorothy Parker

THEORY

Into love and out again,
  Thus I went, and thus I go.
Spare your voice, and hold your pen –
  Well and bitterly I know
All the songs were ever sung,
  All the words were ever said;
Could it be, when I was young,
  Someone dropped me on my head?

Edna St Vincent Millay

INTENTION TO ESCAPE FROM HIM

I think I will learn some beautiful language, useless for commercial
Purposes, work hard at that.
I think I will learn the Latin name of every songbird, not only in
  America but wherever they sing.
(Shun meditation, though; invite the controversial:
Is the world flat? Do bats eat cats?) By digging hard I might deflect that
  river, my mind, that uncontrollable thing.
Turgid and yellow, strong to overflow its banks in spring, carrying
  away bridges;
A bed of pebbles now, through which there trickles one clear narrow
  stream, following a course henceforth nefast –

Dig, dig; and if I come to ledges, blast.

Marilyn Hacker

LANGUEDOCIENNE

For K. J.

This morning the wind came, shaking the quince tree,
making trouble in the chicken yard.

The attic door blew open, windows slammed their casements,
notebooks and envelopes slid off my work-table.

A poplar separating vineyards whispered over
olive and lavender cotton, two shades of summer brown.

Wind makes my head ache. I long for water
surfaces, light on four different river-banks,

silver trembling on the edge, a waterfall
come up inside me as I come down to you.

Early to the train-station; slow bus back through Monday-
shuttered towns;
nectarines under the poplar, wind in the quince tree.

Adrienne Rich

From TWENTY-ONE LOVE POEMS
II

I wake up in your bed. I know I have been dreaming.
Much earlier, the alarm broke us from each other,
you've been at your desk for hours. I know what I dreamed:
our friend the poet comes into my room
where I've been writing for days,
drafts, carbons, poems are scattered everywhere,
and I want to show her one poem
which is the poem of my life. But I hesitate,
and wake. You've kissed my hair
to wake me. *I dreamed you were a poem,*
I say, *a poem I wanted to show someone . . .*
and I laugh and fall dreaming again
of the desire to show you to everyone I love,
to move openly together
in the pull of gravity, which is not simple,
which carries the feathered grass a long way down the upbreathing air.

Lilian Mohin

TRACES, FINE BIRD PRINTS

traces, fine bird prints
above the tide line

do the grains of sand recall
compressing tight to make that shape

or loosening in the new arrangement?

even after waves, somewhere,
my cells remember how it was

your track etching.

Rita Dove

THIS LIFE

The green lamp flares on the table.
You tell me the same thing
as that one,
asleep, upstairs.
Now I see: the possibilities
are golden dresses in a nutshell.

As a child, I fell in love
with a Japanese woodcut
of a girl gazing at the moon.
I waited with her for her lover.
He came in white breeches and sandals.
He had a goatee – he had

your face, though I didn't know it.
Our lives will be the same –
your lips, swollen from whistling
at danger,
and I a stranger
in this desert,
nursing the tough skins of figs.

Alice Notley

MORNINGS

Mornings I wonder if I
can fill my stockings.
By evening I think I
wish I weren't so in love.
Of course I don't wear
stockings. I don't know
anyone who does except for
Darling, & I don't really
know her, the way that
I know you. So may
I say that I had a vision
last night of Heaven?
My stockings were
all that was there.

Mina Loy

From LOVE SONGS TO JOANNES

1

Spawn of Fantasies
Sitting the appraisable
Pig Cupid
His rosy snout
Rooting erotic garbage
'Once upon a time'
Pulls a weed
White star-topped
Among wild oats
Sown in mucous–membrane

I would
An eye in a Bengal light
Eternity in a skyrocket
Constellations in an ocean
Whose rivers run no fresher
Than a trickle of saliva

There are   suspect places

I must live in my lantern
Trimming subliminal flicker
Virginal   to the bellows
Of experience

       Coloured glass

2

The skin–sack
In which a wanton duality
Packed
All the completions
Of my infructuous impulses
Something the shape of a man
To the casual vulgarity of the merely observant
More of a clock–work mechanism
Running down against time
To which I am not paced

My fingertips are numb
from fretting your hair
A God's doormat
On the threshold of your mind

3

We might have coupled
In the bedridden monopoly of a moment
Or broken flesh with one another
At the profane communion table
Where wine is spilled on promiscuous lips

We might have given birth to a butterfly
With the daily news
Printed in blood on its wings

4

Once in a mezzanino
The starry ceiling
Vaulted an unimaginable family
Birdlike abortions
With human throats
And Wisdom's eyes
Who wore lampshade red dresses
And woolen hair

One bore a baby
In a padded porte-enfant
Tied with a sarsenet ribbon
To her goose's wings

But for the abominable shadows
I would have lived
Among their fearful furniture
To teach them to tell me their secrets
Before I guessed
– Sweeping the brood clean out

Helen Dunmore

THE BRIDE'S NIGHTS IN A
STRANGE VILLAGE

At three in the morning
while mist limps between houses
while cloaks and blankets
dampen with dew

the bride sleeps with her husband
bundled in a red blanket,
her mouth parts and a bubble
of sour breathing goes free.
She humps wool up to her ears
while her husband tightens his arms
and rocks her, mumbling. Neither awakes.

In the second month of the marriage
the bride wakes after midnight.
Damp-bodied
she lunges from sleep
hair pricking with sweat
breath knocking her sides.
She eels from her husband's grip
and crouches, listening.

The night is enlarged by sounds.
The rain has started.
It threshes leaves secretively
and there in the blackness
of whining dogs it finds out the house.
Its hiss enfolds her, blots up
her skin, then sifts off, whispering
in her like mirrors
the length of the rainy village.

Maura Stanton

VISIBILITY

I have no illusions.
When I roll towards you at dawn,
I can't see you in the fog.
We've simply memorized each other.
I read a story about a giant
who couldn't see his tiny wife
for all the clouds
drifting around his huge, sad head.
He'd stroke the tops of fir trees
thinking he'd found her hair.
In another version, his wife
turned into an egret,
her strong wings
brushing her husband's face;
then she fell into the sea
weighted down by his immense tear.
Let me tell you this:
I miss your shadow, too,

but I know it waits above the fog
black as the shadow of the oak
you saw in your dream
when you woke up, almost happy.
I know our town's invisible.
The pilots on the way to Alaska
think they're over the sea.
Even if they glimpsed a light
through a rift in the clouds
they'd call it a ship
loaded with timber for the south.
Still, I hear those planes.
Last night on the satellite map
I saw a land without clouds.
Remember, I groped for your hand.
Suppose the men go barefoot?
Suppose the women own fans?

Sappho

BRIDE: MAIDENHOOD, MAIDENHOOD

Bride: Maidenhood, maidenhood, where have you gone and left me?
Maidenhood: No more will I come back to you, no more will
I come back.

Translated by Jane McIntosh Snyder

Helene Johnson

POEM

Little brown boy,
Slim, dark, big-eyed,
Crooning love songs to your banjo
Down at the Lafayette—
Gee, boy, I love the way you hold your head,
High sort of and a bit to one side,
Like a prince, a jazz prince. And I love
Your eyes flashing, and your hands,
And your patent-leathered feet,
And your shoulders jerking the jig-wa.

And I love your teeth flashing,
And the way your hair shines in the spotlight
Like it was the real stuff.
Gee, brown boy, I loves you all over.
I'm glad I'm a jig. I'm glad I can
Understand your dancin' and your
Singin', and feel all the happiness
And joy and don't-care in you.
Gee, boy, when you sing, I can close my ears
And hear tomtoms just as plain.
Listen to me, will you, what do I know
About tomtoms? But I like the word, sort of,
Don't you? It belongs to us.
Gee, boy, I love the way you hold your head,
And the way you sing and dance,
And everything.
Say, I think you're wonderful. You're
All right with me,
You are.

Bessie Smith

DIRTY NO GOODER BLUES

Did you ever fall in love with a man that was no good
Did you ever fall in love with a man that was no good
No matter what you did for him he never understood
The meanest things he could say would thrill you
    through and through

The meanest things he could say would thrill you
    through and through
And there was nothing too dirty for that man to do

He'd treat you nice and kind 'til he'd win your heart in hand
He'd treat you nice and kind 'til he'd win your heart in hand
Then he'd get so cruel that man you just could not stand

Lord, I really don't think no man love can last
Lord, I don't think no man love can last
They love you to death then treat you like a thing of the past

There's nineteen men living in my neighborhood
There's nineteen men living in my neighborhood
Eighteen of them are fools and the one ain't no doggone good

Lord, lord, lord, lord, lord, oh lord, lord lord
That dirty no-good man treats me just like I'm a dog

Georgia Johnson

THE HEART OF A WOMAN

The heart of a woman goes forth with the dawn,
As a lone bird, soft winging, so restlessly on,
Afar o'er life's turrets and vales does it roam
In the wake of those echoes the heart calls home.

The heart of a woman falls back with the night,
And enters some alien cage in its plight,
And tries to forget it has dreamed of the stars
While it breaks, breaks, breaks on the sheltering bars.

Angelina Weld Grimké

AT APRIL

Toss your gay heads,
   Brown girl trees;
Toss your gay lovely heads;
Shake your downy russet curls
All about your brown faces;
Stretch your brown slim bodies;
Stretch your brown slim arms;
Stretch your brown slim toes.
Who knows better than we,
With the dark, dark bodies,
What it means
When April comes a-laughing and a-weeping
Once again
At our hearts?

Elizabeth Spires

PROFIL PERDU

In 1949, in Menton, after long lovemaking
one afternoon, they drew each other:

each kneeling, in turn, by the bed
as the other slept or drifted,

the pen tracing on paper what
the body knew, the strangely lovely

angle of her face thrown back on a hill
of white pillows, and he, in his turn,

wanting if he wants anything never
to leave this room. Each has fallen

softly back into the body as one
might fall into a dream of high blue

meadows in midsummer, midsummer time
leaving them another hour, two,

before they must make their way,
shivering, down the dew-stained mountain.

O let us gently close the door
on love's impromptu sketch and leave

them as we would be left, here
among the long shadows of a room

we have entered without reflection,
all grief or grievance put aside

to draw the body's burning
outline on white sheets, white paper.

Their life, and ours, the evidence.

Janet Gray

UNTITLED

However heavy the walls of love, or well shored, they
barely fail to fall in
on the halls of love.

And on the tables on the porch, how glittering, how
the change of love is handsome
& convincing.

City sacred to love, you are not stale, remove
everything. I can see through
broadcloth & calico

anyway & I will cling, acquisitive, untiring.
I will spit & whip & pull
& cannot be let go.

Norma Cole

From METAMORPHOPSIA

I think of him as a house and as an ordeal
'The house brings the idea of property and connects to
    a cluster of fears concerned with women and desire . . .'
a planet caused the invention of a table, house removed
    veiled blue, dark lady, dark horse
the body constitutes community you can't ellipt it
faith in permission a method or system records how we came
    to be effaced
desperate to conserve matter living and receding

Ingeborg Bachmann

TELL ME, LOVE

Your hat lifts up lightly, says hello, sways in the wind,
your uncovered head has touched the clouds,
your heart has business elsewhere,
your mouth imbibes new languages,
the quaking grass is gaining ground,

summer blows star flowers on and off,
blinded by flakes you raise your face,
you laugh and cry and die by your own hand,
what more can yet befall you –

Tell me, love!

The peacock, in ceremonious amazement, spreads its tail,
the dove pulls up its feather collar,
filled with cooing the air expands,
the duck cries, the whole land eats
wild honey, even in the calm park
every flower bed is bordered with gold dust.

The fish blushes, overtakes the school
and tumbles through grottos into a coral bed.
The scorpion dances shyly to silver sand music.
The beetle smells his lover from afar;
if only I had their sense, I'd also feel
how wings shimmer under their shells
and I'd take the path to distant strawberry patches!

Tell me, love!

Water talks,
the wave takes a wave by the hand,
the grape swells in the vineyard, jumps and falls.
The snail steps so unsuspecting from its house.
A stone knows how to soften a stone!

Tell me, love, what I can't explain:
Should I spend this short, horrid time
with thoughts only, and alone
know no love and give none?
Must one think? Won't he be missed?

You say: another spirit is counting on him . . .
Tell me nothing. I see the salamander
pass through every fire.
No horror hounds him, and he feels no pain.

Translated by Mark Anderson

Catherine Byron

WEDDING AT AUGHRIM,
GALWAY 1900

'A made marriage it was –
my dowry to roof his barn.
Years of sewing and saving
quilts and sheets and shifts
lace from Carrickmacross –
and a fine sum to take
to a family down on its luck.

His mother it was that washed me
that first night
parts of me bruised into bigness
the bites, the scores.
'Alas for the women of this world'
was the word of her keening.

Boys at the well's edge
squeezing frogs in their fists
to pulp.
My brothers pouring oil
down the labourer's flungback nose
to stop his snores.

She brought me my wedding soap
towels with soft nap.
She rocked me in arms
that followed a slower song
than the ceilidh band below.

Boys on the running shore
pressing a limpet's foot
for orange innards.
Boys forking lugworms from the slob
with blunted tines.
Soft bait for lures or frassing.

His mother stands at the door
holding a whip.
Three days and nights
she will not let him come
to his own birthbed
his marriagebed.

        Small boys firing the whin.
        Crack! it's away.
        A burning bush
        no stopping it.'

Kate Ruse-Glason

LOOP

1

We talk upward
against the current
of the downhill waterfall

but there is a point
in us continuing.

We point downhill
but there is talk
against continuing

in us is the current
of an upward waterfall.

2

I woke alone within
the concentric tower.

Everything I say is a lie
but I love the wizard's eyes.

The last line I wrote is true.

The truth alone woke the wizard
love in his eyes.

The last line I wrote
is a lie   everything he says
within the tower is concentric.

Everything the wizard says
is a line   his eyes are last
his lie is concentric.

True   I wrote in his tower
but in love I woke alone.

Solveig von Schoultz

THE RAIN

The rain shook its hair out carelessly over the streets.
I stood in a doorway thinking of you.
The lamp whipped up thin threads of fire
before they plunged blindly to oblivion's foot.
Thus, lit by my heart
the darkness streamed out of you
past past

fallen into the dark.

Translated by Anne Born

Anne Stevenson

HIMALAYAN BALSAM

Orchid–lipped, loose–jointed, purplish, indolent flowers,
with a ripe smell of peaches, like a girl's breath through lipstick,
delicate and coarse in the weedlap of late summer rivers,
dishevelled, weak–stemmed, common as brambles, as love which

subtracts us from seasons, their courtships and murders,
(*Meta segmentata* in her web, and the male waiting,
between blossom and violent blossom, meticulous spiders
repeated in gossamer, and the slim males waiting . . .)

Fragrance too rich for keeping, too light to remember,
like grief for the cat's sparrow and the wild gull's
beach-hatched embryo. (She ran from the reaching water
with the broken egg in her hand, but the clamped bill

refused brandy and grubs, a shred too naked and perilous for
life offered freely in cardboard boxes, little windowsill
coffins for bird death, kitten death, squirrel death, summer
repeated and ended in heartbreak, in the sad small funerals.)

Sometimes, shaping bread or scraping potatoes for supper,
I have stood in the kitchen, transfixed by what I'd call love
if love were a whiff, a wanting for no particular lover,
no child, or baby or creature. 'Love, dear love'

I could cry to these scent-spilling ragged flowers
and mean nothing but 'no', by that word's breadth,
to their evident going, their important descent through red towering
stalks to the riverbed. It's not, as I thought, that death

creates love. More that love knows death. Therefore
tears, therefore poems, therefore the long stone sobs of cathedrals
that speak to no ferret or fox, that prevent no massacre.
(I am combing abundant leaves from these icy shallows.)

Love, it was you who said, 'Murder the killer
we have to call life and we'd be a bare planet under a dead sun.'
Then I loved you with the usual soft lust of October
that says 'yes' to the coming winter and a summoning odour of
    balsam.

H.D. [Hilda Doolittle]

WHITE WORLD

The whole white world is ours,
and the world, purple with rose-bays,
bays, bush on bush,
group, thicket, hedge and tree,
dark islands in a sea
of grey-green olive or wild white-olive,
cut with the sudden cypress shafts,
in clusters, two or three,
or with one slender, single cypress-tree.

Slid from the hill,
as crumbling snow-peaks slide,
citron on citron fill
the valley, and delight
waits till our spirits tire
of forest, grove and bush
and purple flower of the laurel-tree.

Sally Cline

CHANGES

He no longer wears a plait.
He no longer keeps chickens.
The way the Radicals can.
No longer the same person
Or Man.

Now he wears short hair
Now he is the Department's Chairperson
Or Man.

His wife is no longer kept with the chickens.
She runs loose with no shoes.
The way Radical Wives can.
She does not look quite the same person.
Does not act quite according to plan.

He encourages her freedom.
Admires her aplomb.
(He calls her Mom)
He buys her new shoes.
He discovers
She has outgrown them.

He discovers
She has discovered another life.
He discovers
She has discovered
Another
Radical Wife.

Patti Smith

JUDITH 2

yet green eyed golden haired she is not.
she is no angel baby. no candidate for a
glass slipper. she is not the kind of girl
youd find in an eyebrow pencil ad.
no jelly bitch.

but the girl I'd like to touch, we've shared
a bed but I could not touch her. she turned
on her side. I could not touch her. rustling
of new sheets, a very humid memory. but I
could not touch her. nor would she touch me.
plea plead pleading.

victims of the conceit that women were made for
men. radium. I turn out the light. I would not
touch her. after a while desire is overcome.
sooner or later desire hides behind the skin.
retracts, retreats. then sleeps and sleeps and
keeps on sleeping.

Olga Broumas

SLEEPING BEAUTY

I sleep, I sleep
too long,   sheer hours
hound me,   out
of bed and into clothes, I wake
still later, breathless, heart
racing,   sleep
peeling off like a hairless
glutton, momentarily
slaked.   Cold

water shocks me
back from the dream. I see
lovebites like fossils: *something
that did exist*

dreamlike, though
dreams have the perfect alibi, no
fingerprints, evidence
that a mirror could float
back in your own face, gleaming
its silver eye.   Lovebites like fossils. Evidence.
strewn

round my neck like a ceremonial
necklace, suddenly
snapped apart.

O

Blood. Tears. The vital
salt of our body.   Each
other's mouth.
Dreamlike
the taste of you
sharpens my tongue like a thousand shells,
bitter, metallic.   I know

as I sleep
that my blood runs clear
as salt
in your mouth, my eyes.

O

City-center, mid –
traffic, I
wake to your public kiss.   Your name
is Judith, your kiss a sign
to the shocked pedestrians, gathered
beneath the light that means
stop
in our culture
where red is a warning, and men
threaten each other with final violence. *I will drink
your blood.*   Your kiss
is for them
a sign of betrayal, your red
lips suspect, unspeakable
liberties as
we cross the street, kissing
against the light, singing, *This
is the woman I woke from sleep, the woman that woke
me sleeping.*

O

O

Ruth Asher-Pettiphcr

A LOVE LIKE WAR

Du yuh dash that wid luv, Sta. Lureline,
Dat dasheen dat yuh hurling at I?
Is it just feh attrac i attention,
As de pat at yuh gates i go by?

Is it luv an' affection yuh wanting?
Can i hol' yuh so closely tonight?
Or are yuh jus' a feisty big 'oman,
'O is out looking feh a big fight?

When yuh dash out de wata from yuh cooking pan,
And yuh soak i well through to the bone,
Is it jus' as yuh wan feh i to come,
And tek all i clothes off in yuh home?
If dis true, cyan yuh learn to be subtle,
And cort i wid chram and wid grace,
Or are yuh jus' a feisty big 'oman,
Who need a good lick pon de face?

An' i cyan ketch the words that yuh name i,
When i crossing the road at yuh side.
It is Chat fockery, that yuh aiming at me,
Or sweet words from a prospective bride?
Is it luv yuh declaring feh i, gurl,
Or yuh tink as some jegge i am,
Or are yuh jus' a feisty big 'oman,
Who afeared of de big rastaman?

If it luv yuh intentions, my sista,
And yuh feel yuhself sheckray or shy,
Jus' drap i a note, that wid lov, yuh hab wrote,
And not overripe mangoes pon i.
Keep you dawg in him yard feh one secnd,
Jus' to give i a small sporting chance,
Or are yuh jus' a feisty big 'oman,
Who call violence her way of romance?

Marsha Prescod

VICIOUS CIRCLE

He nice frum far, but far frum nice,
He hips dus move like snake.
He make she HOT! Then numb–like ice,
(It more than she could take!)

He born to lie, she born to hear,
He really tell dem sweet!
And if real life try come too near,
She fast go make it fleet.

De bitter blow come quite a shock,
Experience really burned,
The fact he human, weak an bad,
Is hard lesson to learn.

Like soucouyant, he suck she pride,
An leave a harden shell,
So, when a really nice man come,
She *sure* to give him hell!

Dorothy Parker

ONE PERFECT ROSE

A single flow'r he sent me, since we met.
   All tenderly his messenger he chose;
Deep-hearted, pure, with scented dew still wet –
   One perfect rose.

I knew the language of the floweret;
   'My fragile leaves,' it said, 'his heart enclose.'
Love long has taken for his amulet
   One perfect rose.

Why is it no one ever sent me yet
   One perfect limousine, do you suppose?
Ah no, it's always just my luck to get
   One perfect rose.

Grace Nichols

I GO TO MEET HIM

Mornings of dew
and promises

the sound
of bird singing

pink and red
hibiscus kissing

I must devote
some time to the
joy of living

Raising up
from my weeding
of ripening cane

my eyes
make four
with this man

there ain't
no reason
to laugh

but
I laughing
in confusion

his hands
soft his words
quick his lips
curling as in
prayer

I nod

I like this man

Tonight
I go to meet him
like a flame

I see
the trembling star
of murder
in your palm
black man

bleeding
and raging
to death
inside yourself

broken and twisted
as a wheel
watching your blood
run
    thin and saltless
to the earth
as you grip the throat of cane

kin of my skin you are

Iyamide Hazely

BELOVED

I brought my love
wrapped
in cottons and silks
its face and hands
washed
clean as an innocent.
I cupped my hands
for love to drink from,
filled,
filled
with the sweet
mingling

of joy with fear.
I bared the red,
soft,
centre
where my heart had been
to nourish my beloved
and turn the hunger inside
into a field in harvest.

My love was tumbled to the ground
doused with the salt from my own eyes
then tossed aside in a careless gesture.

He who cannot accept a gift of love
does not deserve it.

Ruth Padel

WATERCOURSE

Our window is a drifting smoke
of rainlight, a cage of lichened thorn.
Pale grass, moor walls outside. Inside
there's Schubert song and coffee.
Marooned in Plato's geometric logic,
you sit by the fire,
looking like a nineteenth-century
charcoal sketch. Our daughter is due

in three months. You are sealed
and still. The goldveined eye
of shifting embers,
sound of the piano carrying
a hurt traveller's voice,
our curly dog nuzzling burrs
from her feet on the hearth:
only these move. The bull

who alarmed us yesterday
is a streaming statue
in the farther field.
We are each other's quiet
and concentration. No one
can reach us here.

Christina Rossetti

MONNA INNOMINATA, 4

I loved you first: but afterwards your love,
    Outsoaring mine, sang such a loftier song
As drowned the friendly cooings of my dove.
    Which owes the other most? My love was long,
    And yours one moment seemed to wax more strong;
I loved and guessed at you, you construed me
And loved me for what might or might not be –
    Nay, weights and measures do us both a wrong.
For verily love knows not 'mine' or 'thine';
With separate 'I' and 'thou' free love has done,
    For one is both and both are one in love:
Rich love knows nought of 'thine that is not mine';
    Both have the strength and both the length thereof,
Both of us, of the love which makes us one.

Adrienne Rich

From TWENTY-ONE LOVE POEMS
III

Since we're not young, weeks have to do time
for years of missing each other. Yet only this odd warp
in time tells me we're not young.
Did I ever walk the morning streets at twenty,
my limbs streaming with a purer joy?
did I lean from any window over the city
listening for the future
as I listen here with nerves tuned for your ring?
And you, you move toward me with the same tempo.

Your eyes are everlasting, the green spark
of the blue-eyed grass of early summer,
the green-blue wild cress washed by the spring.
At twenty, yes: we thought we'd live forever.
At forty-five, I want to know even our limits.
I touch you knowing we weren't born tomorrow,
and somehow, each of us will help the other live,
and somewhere, each of us must help the other die.

Sylvia Townsend Warner

UNDER THE SUDDEN BLUE

Under the sudden blue, under the embrace
of the relenting air, under the restored shadow
of the bird flying over the sunny meadow,
the garden ground
preserves an unconvinced and sullen face;
as though
it yet remembered the smite of frost, the wound of snow.
Automatically and without grace
it puts forth monosyllables of green,
answers Yes, or No,
with a muddy daisy, or one celandine,
or in ravel of last year's weeds lies winter-wound.
Poor cadet earth, so clumsy and so slow,
how, labouring with clods, can she keep pace
with Air, the firstborn element, tossing clouds to and fro?

And yet she answers with a spurt
of crocus, and makes light
of snow with snowdrops, and her celandine
is burnished to reflect the sun.

How like your absence and this winter have been!
Long vapours stretched between
me and your light, I saw you bright
beyond them, but your shine
fondled a field not mine.

There was the illumination and there the flight
of shadows black as night;
but I looked round
ever on the same november clear-obscure of dun
and grey and sallow and ash-colour and sere;
even my snows were white
not long, and melted into dirt.
Put out your hand. Feel me. Though the spring is here
I am still cold.

Because of this, because of the winter's hurt,
because I am of the earth element,
dusky, stubborn, retentive, slow to take hold, slow to
        loose hold,
because even to my hair's ends I carry the scent
of peat and of wood-smoke and of leaf-mould,
and because I have been
so long your tillage, so deeply your well-worked ground,
you must be patient;
forgiving my lack of green, my lack of grace,
my stammering blossoms one by one
shoved out, and my face doubtful under the sudden blue,
        under the embrace
of the relenting, of the returning sun.

Liz Lochhead

SUNDAYSONG

its about time
it came back again
if it was going to.
yes   something's nesting
in the tentative creeper scribbling
Kellygreen felt tip
across our bedroom window.
hello.
its a lovely morning.   we've got
full french roast for the enamelled yellow coffee pot.
there'll be transistors in the botanics
and blaring notes of blossom.
let's walk.   let's talk.
let the weekend watch wind down.
let there be sun
let first you and me
and then breakfast and lunch be
rolled into one.

5

'In love I woke alone'

V.R. Lang

A LOVELY SONG FOR JACKSON

If I were a seaweed at the bottom of the sea,
I'd find you, you'd find me.
Fishes would see us and shake their heads
Approvingly from their submarine beds.
Crabs and sea horses would bid us glad cry,
And sea anemone smile us by.
Sea gulls alone would wing and make moan,
Wondering, wondering, where we had gone.

If I were an angel and lost in the sun,
You would be there, and you would be one.
Birds that flew high enough would find us and sing
Gladder to find us than for anything,
And clouds would be proud of us, light everywhere
Would clothe us gold gaily, for dear and for fair.
Trees stretching skyward would see us and smile,
And all over heaven we'd laugh for a while.
Only the fishes would search and make moan,
Wondering, wondering, where we had gone.

Nossis

NOTHING IS SWEETER THAN EROS

Nothing is sweeter than Eros. All other delights
   hold second place – I spit out from my mouth even honey.
Nossis declares this: whoever Cypris has not loved
   does not know what sort of blossoms her roses are.

Translated by Jane McIntosh Snyder

Edna St Vincent Millay

THEME AND VARIATIONS, 1

Not even my pride will suffer much;
Not even my pride at all, maybe,
If this ill-timed, intemperate clutch
Be loosed by you and not by me,
Will suffer; I have been so true
A vestal to that only pride
Wet wood cannot extinguish, nor
Sand, nor its embers scattered, for,
See all these years, it has not died.

And if indeed, as I dare think,
You cannot push this patient flame,
By any breath your lungs could store,
Even for a moment to the floor
To crawl there, even for a moment crawl,
What can you mix for me to drink
That shall deflect me? What you do
Is either malice, crude defense
Of ego, or indifference:
I know these things as well as you;
You do not dazzle me at all.

Some love, and some simplicity.
Might well have been the death of me.

Bernadette Mayer

SONNET

Everyone makes love to their bereft & go
I'd like to know you right this second
But you wouldn't dare come here for the fear
I have of eating this open sandwich I've got
I forget and you've got to I forget & not copy
Tomorrow the two identical different Dutch paintings
Will not look the fruits the way they look today
Thinking of you as if at the beginning of something I do,
                              I will not lie down

You act as if you were married
Thee who comes by whenever you please
I'm not either
You called early, alot to say, I forget
The plot, it was we are alike now it's late
You're asleep   I'm awake

Jessie Redmon Fauset

TOUCHÉ

Dear, when we sit in that high, placid room,
'Loving' and 'doving' as all lovers do,
Laughing and leaning so close in the gloom, –

What is the change that creeps sharp over you?
Just as you raise your fine hand to my hair,
Bringing that glance of mixed wonder and rue?

'Black hair,' you murmur, 'so lustrous and rare,
Beautiful too, like a raven's smooth wing;
Surely no gold locks were ever more fair.'

Why do you say every night that same thing?
Turning your mind to some old constant theme,
Half meditating and half murmuring?

Tell me, that girl of your young manhood's dream,
Her you loved first in that dim long ago –
Had *she* blue eyes? Did *her* hair goldly gleam?

Does *she* come back to you softly and slow,
Stepping wraith-wise from the depths of the past?
Quickened and fired by the warmth of our glow?

There I've divined it! My wit holds you fast.
Nay, no excuses; 'tis little I care.
I knew a lad in my own girlhood's past, –
Blue eyes he had and such waving gold hair!

Elisaveta Bagriana

DESCENDANT

None of my ancestors sat for their portraits,
none of my kin kept a family album
and nothing's come down to me of their precepts,
their faces, their sayings, their lives, their feelings.

But I feel the old and impetuous
blood of the wanderer pulse in my veins.
It wakes me at night, a furious force,
driving me out to commit my first sin.

Maybe some dark-eyed grandmother's mother
dressed in a turban and silks of the harem
eloped in the night with her foreign lover,
ran off in the black with her noble darling.

Maybe a clatter of galloping horses
echoed across the Danubian plain.
Maybe the wind brushed away all traces
and saved them both from the dagger's pain.

This may explain why I go on loving
the breadth of the steppes too vast for the eye,
the dance of the whip, the horse's hard galloping
and snatches of voices the wind hurls to me.

Call me a sinner, beguiler, baiter,
maybe I'll break down midway on life's road.
Nevertheless, I'm yours, your own daughter
and you, my earth-mother, you are my own blood.

Translated by Maxine Kumin

[Unknown] Kisaeng

THE TURKISH BAKERY

I go to the Turkish shop, buy a bun,
An old Turk grasps me by the hand.
If this story is spread abroad,
You alone are to blame, little doll on the shelf.
I will go, yes, go to his bower;
A narrow place, sultry and dark.

I go to the Samjang Temple, light the lantern,
A chief priest grasps me by the hand.
If this story is spread abroad,
You alone are to blame, little altar boy.
I will go, yes, go to his bower;
A narrow place, sultry and dark.

I go to the village well, draw the water,
A dragon within grasps me by the hand.
If this story is spread abroad,
You alone are to blame, O pitcher.
I will go, yes, go to his bower;
A narrow place, sultry and dark.

I go to the tavern, buy the wine,
An innkeeper grasps me by the hand.
If this story is spread abroad,
You alone are to blame, O wine jug.
I will go, yes, go to his bower;
A narrow place, sultry and dark.

Translated by Peter H. Lee

Anna Akhmatova

I SEE, I SEE THE CRESCENT
MOON

I see, I see the crescent moon
through the willow's thick foliage.
I hear, I hear the regular beat
of unshod hooves.

You don't want to sleep either?
In a year you weren't able to forget me,
you're not used to finding
your bed empty?

Don't I talk with you
in the sharp cries of falcons?
Don't I look into your eyes
from the matt, white pages?

Why do you circle round,
the silent house like a thief?
Or do you remember the agreement
and wait for me alive?

I am falling asleep. The moon's blade
cuts through the stilling dark.
Again hoofbeats. It is my own warm
heart that beats so.

Translated by Richard McKane

Ntozake Shange

GET IT & FEEL GOOD

you cd just take what
he's got for you
i mean what's available
cd add up in the long run
if it's music/ take it
say he's got good

dishwashing techniques
he cd be a marvelous
masseur/ take it
whatever good there is to
get/ get it & feel good

say there's an electrical
wiring fanatic/ he cd
come in handy some day
suppose they know how to tend plants
if you want somebody
with guts/ you cd go to a rodeo
a prize fight/ or a gang war might be up your alley
there's somebody out there
with something you want/
not alla it/ but a lil
bit from here & there can
add up in the long run

whatever good there is to get
get it & feel good
this one's got kisses
that one can lay
linoleum
this one likes wine
that one fries butter fish
real good
this one is a anarcho-musicologist
this one wants pushkin to rise again
& that one has had it with the past tense/
whatever good there is to get/
get it & feel good
this one cd make music
roll around the small of
yr back & that one jumps
up & down in the gardens
it cd be yrs
there really is enuf to get
by with in this world but
you have to know what yr looking

for/ whatever good there is to get
get it & feel good
you have to know what
they will give up easily
what's available is not always
all that's possible
but there's so much fluctuation
in the market these days
you have to be
particular
whatever good there is to get
get it & feel good

whatever good there is to get
get it & feel good/ get it & feel good
snatch it & feel good
grab it & feel good
steal it & feel good
borrow it & feel good
reach it & feel good
you cd
        oh yeah
            & feel good.

Margaret Atwood

EVENTUAL PROTEUS

I held you
through all your shifts
of structure: while your bones turned
from caved rock back to marrow,
the dangerous
fur faded to hair
the bird's cry died in your throat
the treebark paled from your skin
the leaves from your eyes

till you limped back again
to daily man:
a lounger on streetcorners
in iron-shiny gabardine
a leaner on stale tables;
at night a twitching sleeper
dreaming of crumbs and rinds and a sagging woman
caged by a sour bed.

The early
languages are obsolete.

These days we keep
our weary distances:
sparring in the vacant spaces
of peeling rooms
and rented minutes, climbing
all the expected stairs, our voices
abraded with fatigue,
our bodies wary.

Shrunk by my disbelief
you cannot raise
the green gigantic skies, resume
the legends of your disguises:
this shape is final.

Now, when you come near
attempting towards me across
these sheer cavernous
inches of air

your flesh has no more stories
or surprises;

my face flinches
under the sarcastic
tongues of your estranging
fingers,
the caustic remark of your kiss.

Grace Nichols

LOVEACT

She enter into his Great House
her see-far looking eyes
unassuming

He fix her with his glassy stare
and feel the thin fire in his blood
awakening

Soon she is the fuel
that keep them all going

He/his mistresswife/ and his
children who take to her breasts
like leeches

He want to tower above her
want her to raise her ebony
haunches and when she does
he think she can be trusted
and drinks her in

and his mistresswife
spending her days in rings
of vacant smiling
is glad to be rid of the
loveact

But time pass/es

Her sorcery cut them
like a whip

She hide her triumph
and slowly stir the hate
of poison in

Fanny Howe

BUT I, TOO, WANT TO BE
A POET

But I, too, want to be a poet
and live a virtuous life
To erase from my days
confusion & poverty
fiction & a sharp tongue!

To sing again
with the tones of adolescence
demanding vengeance
against my enemies, with words
clear & austere

To end this tumultuous quest
for reasonable solutions
to situations mysterious & sore

To have the height to view
myself as I view others
with lenience and love

To be free of the need
to make a waste of money
when my passion,
first and last,
is for the ecstatic lash
of the poetic line
and no visible recompense.

Stevie Smith

AT SCHOOL

A Paolo and Francesca situation but more hopeful, say in Purgatory

At school I always walk with Elwyn
Walk with Elwyn all the day
Oh my darling darling Elwyn
We shall never go away.

This school is a most curious place
Everything happens faintly
And the other boys and girls who are here
We cannot see distinctly.

All the day I walk with Elwyn
And sometimes we also ride
Both of us would always really
Rather be outside.

Most I like to ride with Elwyn
In the early morning sky
Under the solitary mosses
That hang from the trees awry.

The wind blows cold then
And the wind comes to the dawn
And we ride silently
And kiss as we ride down.

Oh my darling darling Elwyn
Oh what a sloppy love is ours
Oh how this sloppy love sustains us
When we get back to the school bars.

There are bars round this school
And inside the lights are always burning bright
And yet there are shadows
That belong rather to the night than to the light.

Oh my darling darling Elwyn
Why is there this dusty heat in this closed school?
All the radiators must be turned full on
Surely that is against the rules?

Hold my hand as we run down the long corridors
Arched over with tombs
We are underground now a long way
Look out, we are getting close to the boiler room.

We are not driven harshly to the lessons you know
That go on under the electric lights
That go on persistently, patiently you might say,
They do not mind if we are not very bright.

Open this door quick, Elwyn, it is break-time
And if we ride quickly we can come to the sea-pool
And swim; will not that be a nice thing to do?
Oh my darling do not look so sorrowful.

Oh why do we cry so much
Why do we not go to some place that is nice?
Why do we only stand close
And lick the tears from each other's eyes?

Darling, my darling
You are with me in the school and in the dead trees' glade
If you were not with me
I should be afraid.

Fear not the ragged dawn skies
Fear not the heat of the boiler room
Fear not the sky where it flies
The jagged clouds in their rusty colour.

Do not tell me not to cry my love
The tears run down your face too
There is still half an hour left
Can we not think of something to do?

Ida Cox

WILD WOMEN BLUES

I've got a different system
And a way of my own,
When my man starts kicking
I let him find another home.
I get full of good liquor
And walk the street all night,
Go home and put my man out
If he don't treat me right,
Wild women don't worry,
Wild women don't have the blues.

You never get nothing
By being an angel child,
You better change your ways
And get real wild.
I want to tell you something
I wouldn't tell you no lie,
Wild women are the only kind
That really get by,
'Cause wild women don't worry,
Wild women don't have the blues.

Lucille Clifton

SISTERS

me and you be sisters.
we be the same.
me and you
coming from the same place.
me and you
be greasing our legs
touching up our edges.
me and you
be scared of rats
be stepping on roaches.
me and you
come running high down purdy street one time

and mama laugh and shake her head at
me and you.
me and you
got babies
got thirty-five
got black
let out hair go back
be loving ourselves
be loving ourselves
be sisters.
only where you sing
i poet.

Eibhlín Dhubh ní Chonaill

From THE LAMENT FOR ARTHUR O'LEARY

My love forever!
The day I first saw you
At the end of the market-house,
My eye observed you,
My heart approved you,
I fled from my father with you.
Far from my home with you.

I never repented it:
You whitened a parlour for me.
Painted rooms for me,
Reddened ovens for me,
Baked fine bread for me,
Basted meat for me,
Slaughtered beasts for me;
I slept in ducks' feathers
Till midday milking-time,
Or more if it pleased me.

My friend forever!
My mind remembers
That fine spring day
How well your hat suited you,

Bright gold banded,
Sword silver-hilted –
Right hand steady –
Threatening aspect –
Trembling terror
On treacherous enemy –
You poised for a canter
On your slender bay horse.
The Saxons bowed to you,
Down to the ground to you,
Not for love of you
But for deadly fear of you,
Though you lost your life to them,
Oh my soul's darling.

My friend you were forever!
I knew nothing of your murder
Till your horse came to the stable
With the reins beneath her trailing,
And your heart's blood on her shoulders
Staining the tooled saddle
Where you used to sit and stand.
My first leap reached the threshold,
My second reached the gateway,
My third leap reached the saddle.

I struck my hands together
And I made the bay horse gallop
As fast as I was able,
Till I found you dead before me
Beside a little furze-bush.
Without Pope or bishop,
Without priest or cleric
To read the death-psalms for you,
But a spent old woman only
Who spread her cloak to shroud you –
Your heart's blood was still flowing:
I did not stay to wipe it
But filled my hands and drank it.

My friend and my treasure!
It's bad treatment for a hero
To lie hooded in a coffin,
The warm-hearted rider
That fished in bright rivers,
That drank in great houses
With white-breasted women.
My thousand sorrows
That I've lost my companion.

My love and my dear!
Your stooks are standing,
Your yellow cows milking;
On my heart is such sorrow
That all Munster could not cure it,
Nor the wisdom of the sages.
Till Art O'Leary returns
There will be no end to the grief
That presses down on my heart,
Closed up tight and firm
Like a trunk that is locked
And the key is mislaid.

All you women out there weeping,
Wait a little longer;
We'll drink to Art son of Connor
And the souls of all the dead,
Before he enters the school –
Not learning wisdom or music
But weighed down by earth and stones.

Translated by Eilís Dillon

Madge Herron

POEM FOR FRANCIS HARVEY

Christ, and when I sleep
Your wounds hop on to me
like little mice:
what encumbrance is this?
Survive the night

and be my finest poem
pushed thinly through
and nothing of you spilt.
A legend in a vessel;
twixt the gable
and the well
whortled darkening stones
near where you fell
I hear Him coming
in the mass.
Will He love me?
who am the Bull –
and will He say?
There's not a day
goes past
But I think on thee,
My Love, My Love.

Elizabeth Barrett Browning

A MAN'S REQUIREMENTS

I

Love me Sweet, with all thou art,
　　Feeling, thinking, seeing;
Love me in the lightest part,
　　Love me in full being.

II

Love me with thine open youth
　　In its frank surrender;
With the vowing of thy mouth,
　　With its silence tender.

III

Love me with thine azure eyes,
　　Made for earnest granting;
Taking colour from the skies,
　　Can Heaven's truth be wanting?

IV

Love me with their lids, that fall
   Snow-like at first meeting;
Love me with thine heart, that all
   Neighbours then see beating.

V

Love me with thine hand stretched out
   Freely – open-minded:
Love me with thy loitering foot, –
   Hearing one behind it.

VI

Love me with thy voice, that turns
   Sudden faint above me;
Love me with thy blush that burns
   When I murmur *Love me!*

VII

Love me with thy thinking soul,
   Break it to love-sighing;
Love me with thy thoughts that roll
   On through living – dying.

VIII

Love me in thy gorgeous airs,
   When the world has crowned thee;
Love me, kneeling at thy prayers,
   With the angels round thee.

IX

Love me pure, as musers do,
   Up the woodlands shady:
Love me gaily, fast and true,
   As a winsome lady.

X

Through all hopes that keep us brave,
    Farther off or nigher,
Love me for the house and grave,
    And for something higher.

XI

Thus, if thou wilt prove me, Dear,
    Woman's love no fable,
I will love *thee* – half a year –
    As a man is able.

Gwendolyn Brooks

LOVE NOTE
I: SURELY

Surely you stay my certain own, you stay
My you. All honest, lofty as a cloud.
Surely I could come now and find you high,
As mine as you ever were; should not be awed.
Surely your word would pop as insolent
As always: 'Why, of course I love you, dear.'
Your gaze, surely, ungauzed as I could want.
Your touches, that never were careful, what they were.
Surely – But I am very off from that.
From surely. From indeed. From the decent arrow
That was my clean naïveté and my faith.
This morning men deliver wounds and death.
They will deliver death and wounds tomorrow.
And I doubt all. You. Or a violet.

Sulpicia

IT IS PLEASING

It is pleasing – the fact that in your carefree way you allow
    yourself so much on my behalf, lest I suddenly take a bad
      fall.
So you care more for a skirt – a wench loaded down with
    her wool-basket – than for Sulpicia, daughter of Servius.
There are people concerned about me, and they especially
    worry
        that I might give way to that lowly mistress of yours.

Translated by Jane McIntosh Snyder

Ma Rainey

DON'T FISH IN MY SEA

My daddy come home this morning
Drunk as he could be
My daddy come home this morning
Drunk as he could be
I knowed by that, he's
Done gone bad on me
He used to stay out late, now
He don't come home at all
He used to stay out late, now
He don't come home at all
(No kidding, either.)
I know there's another mule
Been kicking in my stall

If you don't like my ocean
Don't fish in my sea
Don't like my ocean
Don't fish in my sea
Stay out of my valley
And let my mountain be

I ain't had no loving
Since god knows when
I ain't had no loving
Since god knows when
That's the reason I'm through with these
No good trifling men

You'll never miss the sunshine
Till the rain begin to fall
Never miss the sunshine
Till the rain begin to fall
You'll never miss your ham till a–
Nother mule be in your stall

Sylvia Townsend Warner

DRAWING YOU, HEAVY WITH SLEEP . . .

Drawing you, heavy with sleep to lie closer,
Staying your poppy head upon my shoulder,
It was as though I pulled the glide
Of a full river to my side.

Heavy with sleep and with sleep pliable
You rolled at a touch towards me. Your arm fell
Across me as a river throws
An arm of flood across meadows.

And as the careless water its mirroring sanction
Grants to him at the river's brim long stationed,
Long drowned in thought, that yet he lives
Since in that mirroring tide he moves,

Your body lying by mine to mine responded:
Your hair stirred on my mouth, my image was dandled
Deep in your sleep that flowed unstained
On from the image entertained.

Gill Vickers

SUN

since we said politely   thankyou
we did not need each other in our faces
anymore   became conducive to fine defeat

like corrugated cardboard
I wished to fold up
and put myself away

watch out   you said   and
fell, unable to
unfold your arms
to catch your body

and I repeated you.

Failing softly with all we knew
the diluted touch
of any other body

Charlotte Mew

ON THE ROAD TO THE SEA

We passed each other, turned and stopped for half an hour, then went our way,
        I who make other women smile did not make you –
But no man can move mountains in a day.
        So this hard thing is yet to do.

But first I want your life: – before I die I want to see
        The world that lies behind the strangeness of your eyes,
There is nothing gay or green there for my gathering, it may be,
        Yet on brown fields there lies
A haunting purple bloom: is there not something in grey skies
        And in grey sea?
        I want what world there is behind your eyes,
        I want your life and you will not give it me.

Now, if I look, I see you walking down the years,
Young, and through August fields – a face, a thought, a swinging dream
perched on a stile – ;
I would have liked (so vile we are !) to have taught you tears
But most to have made you smile.

To-day is not enough or yesterday: God sees it all –
Your length on sunny lawns, the wakeful rainy nights – ; tell me – ; (how vain
to ask), but it is not a question – just a call – ;
Show me then, only your notched inches climbing up the garden wall,
I like you best when you are small.

Is this a stupid thing to say
Not having spent with you one day?
No matter; I shall never touch your hair
Or hear the little tick behind your breast,
Still it is there,
And as a flying bird
Brushes the branches where it may not rest
I have brushed your hand and heard
The child in you: I like that best

So small, so dark, so sweet; and were you also then too grave and wise?
Always I think. Then put your far off little hand in mine: – Oh! let it
rest;
I will not stare into the early world beyond the opening eyes,
Or vex or scare what I love best.
But I want your life before mine bleeds away –
Here – not in heavenly hereafters – soon, –
I want your smile this very afternoon,
(The last of all my vices, pleasant people used to say,
I wanted and I sometimes got – the Moon!)

You know, at dusk, the last bird's cry,
And round the house the flap of the bat's low flight,
Trees that go black against the sky
And then – how soon the night!

No shadow of you on any bright road again,
And at the darkening end of this – what voice? whose kiss? As if you'd say!
It is not I who have walked with you, it will not be I who take away
Peace, peace, my little handful of the gleaner's grain
From your reaped fields at the shut of day.

Peace! Would you not rather die
Reeling, – with all the cannons at your ear?
So, at least, would I,
And I may not be here
To-night, to-morrow morning or next year.
Still I will let you keep your life a little while,
See dear?
I have made you smile.

Nina Cassian

ACCIDENT

The light collides with the walls, bounces off,
slips into a glass, leaps out choking,
hits my eyeballs with a faint, painful clang,
and then takes a step or two backwards, goes for
your glassy-smooth mouth, and shatters it.
Your mouth is patterned with black veining.
We both have serious injuries.
The light is imitating our blood.

Translated by Fleur Adcock

Audre Lorde

SISTERS IN ARMS

The edge of our bed was a wide grid
where your 15 year old daughter was hanging
gut-sprung on police wheels
a cablegram nailed to the wood
next to a map of the Western Reserve
I could not return with you to bury the body
reconstruct your nightly cardboards
against the seeping Transvaal cold
I could not plant the other limpet mine
against a wall at the railroad station
nor carry either of your souls back from the river
in a calabash upon my head
so I bought you a ticket to Durban
on my American Express

and we lay together
in the first light of a new season.

Now clearing roughage from my autumn garden
cow-sorrel over-grown rocket gone to seed
I reach for a taste of today
the New York Times finally mentions your country
a half-page story
of the first white south african killed in the 'unrest'
Not of Black children massacred at Sebonkeng
six-year-olds imprisoned for threatening the state
not of Thabo Sibeko, first-grader, in his own blood
on his grandmother's parlour floor
Joyce, nine, trying to crawl to him
shitting through her navel
not of a three week old infant, nameless
lost under the burned beds of Tembisa
my hand comes down like a brown vise over the marigolds
reckless through despair
we were two Black women touching our flame
and we left our dead behind us
I hovered   you rose   the last ritual of healing
   'It is spring,' you whispered
   'I sold the ticket for guns and sulfur
   I leave for home tomorrow'
and where ever I touch you
I lick cold from my fingers
taste rage
like salt from the lips of a woman
who has killed too often to forget
and carries each death in her eyes
your mouth a parting orchid
   'Someday you will come to *my* country
   and we will fight side by side?'

Keys jingle in my passageway   threatening
whatever is coming belongs here
I reach for your sweetness
but silence explodes like a pregnant belly
into my face
a vomit of nevers.

Mmanthatisi* turns away from the cloth
her daughters-in-law are dyeing
the baby drools milk from her breast
she hands him half-asleep to his sister
dresses again for war
knowing the men will follow.
In the intricate Maseru† twilights
quick   sad   vital
she maps the next day's battle
dreams of Durban‡ sometimes
visions the deep wry song of beach pebbles
running after the sea

*M-man-tha-tisi: warrior queen and leader of the Tlokwa (Sotho)
people during the *mfecane* (crushing), one of the greatest crises in
southern African history. Sotho now lives in the Orange Free State,
SA.
†Ma-se-ru: scene of a great Tlokwa battle and now the capital of
Lesotho.
‡Durban: Indian Ocean seaport and resort area in Natal Province, SA.

Michelene Wandor

From COURTLY LOVE

So Christopher Columbus was a Jew
doesn't this give you
a whole new view
of an old world

in 1492 Isabella took her new name
from a safe queen
in Spain
and what better way
to pass for real – temporarily
that is, until a new shore
releases an old name

she, playing the psaltery
a befitting and delicate sound
for a woman
stringing the others along
while in secret she
puffed out her cheeks
performed clandestine loving
with the sackbutt
a secret
closet fipple flute lover
cornet on the corniche
a cherub with perfect pitch
not an eyelash out of scale

one day the troubadour arrived
short hair spiked green
round the head, ears curious
to the world, a jagged
prickly pear
from a far-off desert
Babylonia or Persia
travelled from
the heat of southern Spain
across the Tuscan wilds

the troubadour has disguised the music
the troubadour has disguised shape
the troubadour has disguised belief
the troubadour observes
that the monk is in love with the monk
that the woman musician is disguised as a man
that the Pope has just had a baby
that the eunuch is in love with the troubadour
for they make music and little else

that fair white hand which pierces my heart
can also heal me, sings
the eunuch
take up thy lute and walk, thinks the troubadour

Louise Labé

YOU ARE ALONE MY EVIL AND MY GOOD

You are alone my evil and my good
With you I have everything – without you nothing.

Translated by Helen R. Lane

Mei-Mei Berssenbrugge

THE STAR FIELD

Placing our emotion on a field, I said, became a nucleus of space,
defined by a rain of light and indeterminate contours of a landscape,
like the photograph of an explosion, and gave the travel of your gaze
                                        into it, or on me,
imaginative weight of the passage along a gulf of space
or a series of aluminum poles.

She walks through rooms of blue chain-linked fence, a spacious tennis
                                        court
of rooms on concrete, instead of the single movement of a room,
                                        where sky and earth
would come together.

Outside is the field she is thinking about: a category of gray dots
on a television screen of star data, representing no one's experience,
but which thrills all who gaze on it, so it must be experience. And
the land at large becomes the light on the land.

A coyote or a flicker's call
is transfixed at the moment before its dissemination across the field,
a sediment of, instead
of the trace of feeling, the ratio of people to the space.
I pass through blue focal planes, a scene of desire.

The material of the sky adjacent to me eludes me, a pure signifier,
shifting sense, the sky or space a gradation of material, the light
a trace of mobility like a trace of light on a sensitive screen,
extended into the plane of the trace
and marked by light poles or drawn close by a planet at the edge.

Your name becomes a trace of light. Through
its repetition and deferral, my life protects itself
from blurs, time lapses, flares
of the sexual act, its mobility of an afterimage.

Then I can understand the eye's passage into depth
as an inability to stand still for you to see.

Marie de France

LOVE IS A WOUND WITHIN
THE BODY

Love is a wound within the body
That has no outward sign.

Translated by Helen R. Lane

Chase Twichell

PHYSICS

Think of the present as a splitting atom
one-half weighted, out of kilter,
trailing its roots and trash,
and then the liquid glamour of the other,
swimming forward into foreign darkness
and the soft folds of space.
If fate is a chromosome,
a man and a woman might be
capable of genetic love.

No one leaves for heaven anymore,
that ill-lit, inhospitable
planet the color of eggshell,
sick with candles and flowers.
It empties itself of all things outlandish,
that is its purpose.
It crushes the fossil stars
for its fuel, clogging the sky
with their dessicated seed.

One human body, female, shudders.
Think of her pleasure as a tiny engine
or a unit of generated energy.
As something for nothing.
All over the earth the separate sparks
flash quietly, with exquisite frailty.
A body holding more of a charge
would come apart like the fractured atom,
and heaven, inverted, be used
as a bin for the debris.

When the music forces sadness on us,
the coincidence of joy unnerves us,
and the sexual lights flare up,
we drift into a universe of disasters
holding our slight, impractical instruments,
navigating by instinct,
as though that could save us.

You know what happens.
We survive straight through to the end.
We lie down together
on a hard, familiar bed
though each of us has been
already once or twice
a godsend to someone else.
Let love infect and reinfect us,
and endure in our blood
as a code of bright cells,
holy and incurable.

Alice Walker

DID THIS HAPPEN TO YOUR MOTHER?
DID YOUR SISTER THROW UP A LOT?

I love a man who is not worth
my love.
Did this happen to your mother?
Did your grandmother wake up
for no good reason
in the middle of the night?

I thought love could be controlled.
It cannot.
Only behavior can be controlled.
By biting your tongue purple
rather than speak.·
Mauling your lips.
Obliterating his number
too thoroughly
to be able to phone.

Love has made me sick.

Did your sister throw up a lot?
Did your cousin complain
of a painful knot
in her back?
Did your aunt always
seem to have something else
troubling her mind?

I thought love would adapt itself
to my needs.
But needs grow too fast;
they come up like weeds.
Through cracks in the conversation.
Through silences in the dark.
Through everything you thought was concrete.

Such needful love has to be chopped out
or forced to wilt back,
poisoned by disapproval
from its own soil.

This is bad news, for the conservationist.

My hand shakes before this killing.
My stomach sits jumpy in my chest.
My chest is the Grand Canyon
sprawled empty
over the world.

Whoever he is, he is not worth all this.

And I will never
unclench my teeth long enough
to tell him so.

Eunice de Souza

FROM YOU I HAVE UNDERSTOOD

From you I have understood
something of the silence of gods
how they tire of being the first cause
of every quarrel
how they shrink
from sweaty importunity.
Even the skies these days
are full of junk in orbit.

Be less like the wild gods, love.

Song of Solomon*

CHAPTER 3

By night on my bed I sought him whom my soul
loveth: I sought him, but I found him not.

2 I will rise now, and go about the city in the streets, and
in the broad ways I will seek him whom my soul loveth:
I sought him, but I found him not.

3 The watchmen that go about the city found me: to
whom I said, Saw ye him whom my soul loveth?

4 It was but a little that I passed from them, but I found
him whom my soul loveth: I held him, and would not
let him go, until I had brought him into my mother's
house, and into the chamber of her that conceived me.

5 I charge you, O ye daughters of Jerusalem, by the
roes, and by the hinds of the field, that ye stir not up,
nor awake my love, till he please.

6 Who is this that cometh out of the wilderness like
pillars of smoke, perfumed with myrrh and
frankincense, with all powders of the merchant?

7 Behold his bed, which is Solomon's; threescore valiant
men are about it, of the valiant of Ĭs'rā–ĕl.

8 They all hold swords, being expert in war: every man
hath his sword upon his thigh because of fear in the
night.

9 King Solomon made himself a chariot of the wood of
Lebanon.

10 He made the pillars thereof of silver, the bottom
thereof of gold, the covering of it of purple, the midst
thereof being paved with love, for the daughters of
Jerusalem.

11 Go forth, O ye daughters of Zion, and behold King
Solomon with the crown wherewith his mother
crowned him in the day of his espousals, and in the day
of the gladness of his heart.

*Anon [The Bible, King James' version]

Gertrude Stein

From A SONATINA FOLLOWED BY ANOTHER

She is that kind of a wife. She can see.

And a credit to me.

And a credit to me she is sleepily a credit to me and what do I credit her with I credit her with a kiss.

    1. Always sweet.

    2. Always right.

    3. Always welcome.

    4. Always wife.

    5. Always blessed.

    6. Always a successful druggist of the second class and we know what that means. Who credits her with all this a husband with a kiss and what is he to be always more lovingly his missus' help and hero. And when is he heroic, well we know when.

Win on a foul pretty as an owl pretty as an owl win on a fowl. And the fowl is me and she is pretty as an owl. Battling Siki and Capridinks capridinks is pretty and winks, winks of sleep and winks of love. Capridinks. Capridinks is my love and my Coney.

Sulpicia

FINALLY A LOVE HAS COME

Finally a love has come which would cause me more shame
    were Rumor to conceal it rather than lay it bare for all.
Won over by my Muses, the Cytherean goddess [Venus]
  brought me
    him, and placed him in my bosom.
Venus has discharged her promise; if anyone is said
    to have had no joys of his own, let him tell of mine.
I would not wish to entrust anything to sealed tablets,
    lest anyone read my words before my lover does.
But I delight in my wayward ways and loathe to dissemble
    for fear of Rumor. Let me be told of:
I am a worthy woman who has been together
    with a worthy man.

Gillian Allnutt

MEETING YOU AT AN UNDERGROUND STATION

we meet
on the dot
of eight

you wait

tight little
knots of love
like buttons
close your coat
from boots to throat

your eye takes note
of time. O not
a measurement of spoons –
the way the moon holds
up a winter night for
just so long –
but clock and date
a london transport
ticket check

did you really think
I would be late?
it's not as simple as that

you write

I wait

beside my bicycle
unriled, fish out
deliberate respect
for words that
might drop out
of the moon's
shut mouth at
any moment –

I keep it in my pocket
with my cigarettes

somewhere
here I've got it
with the dirty handkerchief
the tuppeny bits
the chocolate wrapper
twisted tight and obsolete –
make it as little as possible
before you throw it out
the chocolate tasted
bittersweet
and made me fat
I didn't really want it
but I had to wait
somewhere

you with your body
bent into a bit
of notebook
and your tongue thin
as a ball point pen
perhaps you only write
'do not forget
to put the cat out
of the kitchen door
tonight' to take me in

you've still got your gloves on
how can you properly write?

is this a falling out
of love? is this quite
what we meant within
the sweet short sight
of the moon insensible
with summer? do you remember
how we ate light by water

out of a runcible spoon
that night when all
the *stars* came undone
like buttons?
it's time to do
things up. to part
to put a full stop
after what is written

O you
and your hermetic art
don't shut me out
when you could change
a tuppeny bit
into the moon

'don't phone me up
tonight or any night'

we stand apart
before the barrier
debate a button
all alone

we've missed the last train
to the moon

Lady Anne Lindsay

AULD ROBIN GRAY

When the sheep are in the fauld, and the kye at hame
and a' the warld to rest are gane,
The waes o' my heart fa' in showers frae my e'e,
While my gudeman lies close to me.

Young Jamie lo'ed me weel, and sought me for his bride;
But saving a croun he had naething else beside:
To make the croun a pund, young Jamie gaed to sea;
And the croun and the pund were baith for me.

He hadna been awa' a week but only twa,
When my father brak his arm, and the cow was stown awa';
My mother she fell sick, – and my Jamie at the sea –
And auld Robin Gray came a-courtin' me.

My father couldna work, and my mother couldna spin;
I toiled day and night, but their bread I couldna win;
Auld Rob maintained them baith, and wi' tears in his e'e
Said, 'Jennie, for their sakes, O marry me.'

My heart it said nay; I looked for Jamie back;
But the wind it blew high, and the ship it was a wrack;
His ship it was a wrack – Why didna Jamie dee?
Or why do I live to cry, Wae's me!

My father urged me sair: my mother didna speak;
But she look'd in my face till my heart was like to break:
They gi'ed him my hand, tho my heart was in the sea;
Sae auld Robin Gray he was gudeman to me.

I hadna been a wife a week but only four,
When mournfu' as I sat on the stane at the door,
I saw my Jamie's wraith – for I couldna think it he,
Till he said, 'I'm come hame to marry thee.'

O sair, sair did we greet, and muckle did we say;
We took but ae kiss, and tore ourselves away:
I wish that I were dead, but I'm no like to dee;
And why was I born to say, Wae's me!

I gang like a ghaist, and I carena to spin;
I daurna think on Jamie, for that wad be a sin;
But I'll do my best a gude wife aye to be,
For auld Robin Gray he is kind to me.

Alicia Suskin Ostriker

EXTRATERRESTRIAL

A Wedding Poem for Nina and John, January 2, 1989

> Do the angels really
> reabsorb only the radiance that streamed out from themselves,
> or sometimes, as if by an oversight, is there a trace of our
> essence, in it as well?
>   Rilke, *Second Duino Elegy*

Nina and John: there are spaceships circling above us
This afternoon in the raw of winter, the early
Dawn of a new year,

There are extraterrestrial visitors thoughtfully watching
Our cerulean sphere spin through the void. As they monitor
Our little destinies,

If they are able to shiver they do so, hugging
Their bodies, if they have bodies. To them we are
Perfectly lovely,

A bluegreen marble that any boy would be happy
To keep in his pocket. They watch us pursue our orderly
Orbit around the

Local star upon which our lives completely
Depend, they enjoy our cooling and warming, they clap
Their hands to see it

If they have hands – or maybe they clap their feelers
Or wave their antennae – they find us a
Charming spectacle.

And best of all, with their expanded senses,
More powerful than our own, with their subtlety able
To pick up fainter

Signals, and also different *sorts* of signals,
Not only melodious optic, thundering ultraviolet,
Stridulous X-rays –

Their receptors can pick up what William Blake
Used to call 'beams of love:' those emanations
Emitted by lovers,

That fly from the planet like molecules lighter than air,
Or rather zap from it, waves more potent than lasers
Pulsing their message:

We have formed a unit, people, we're loving each other,
We are doing it now, can you read us, it's
What we were born for.

To our visitors, such signals are like fireflies
On a summer evening, so pretty, and they like to
Sense the gradations.

Pure sex – is a basic best, a kind of percussion.
Sex with love, a more eloquent flashing, a richer
Combination of wavelengths.

The most glorious signal of course is that transmitted
By married lovers, for this one is perfect art
Allied to nature.

It says: *We're loving, we're working at it, it's like*
Climbing up Everest, we're playing, it's
Really sensational,

Different from everything else, it overwhelms us,
Seems to be making us stronger, more alive,
But also weaker –

Difficult, dangerous life, we are up to our eyeballs
In it, we'll never stop. And the visitors look at each other –
Nina and John, are you paying careful attention –

Smiling, applauding, the way we all do when children
Learning a skill perform some feat that is difficult,
Since learning to love is something

Like learning to walk, or swim, or ride a bicycle,
It's like writing poems, and maybe like writing history,
– Hard, but rewarding.

Go, say the visitors, mentally egging them on.
You're getting it, yes, you've got it, you can do it,
Congratulations.

They add their wishes to ours. Young man, young woman,
All of us wish you joy, in sex, in love,
And of course in marriage.

I'm calling them visitors, picturing them in spaceships . . .
Who are they really? Maybe Rilke was right,
Maybe they're angels.

Anna Wickham

NERVOUS PROSTRATION

I married a man of the Croydon class
When I was twenty-two.
And I vex him, and he bores me
Till we don't know what to do!
It isn't good form in the Croydon class
To say you love your wife,
So I spend my days with the tradesmen's books
And pray for the end of life.

In green fields are blossoming trees
And a golden wealth of gorse,
And young birds sing for joy of worms:
It's perfectly clear, of course,
That it wouldn't be taste in the Croydon class
To sing over dinner or tea:
But I sometimes wish the gentleman
Would turn and talk to me!

But every man of the Croydon class
Lives in terror of joy and speech.
'Words are betrayers,' 'Joys are brief' –
The maxims their wise ones teach –
And for all my labour of love and life
I shall be clothed and fed,
And they'll give me an orderly funeral
When I'm still enough to be dead.

6

'Your name on my tongue'

Emily Dickinson

AH, TENERIFFE!

Ah, Teneriffe!
Retreating Mountain!
Purples of Ages – pause for *you* –
Sunset – reviews her Sapphire Regiment –
Day – drops you her Red Adieu!

Still – Clad in your Mail of ices –
Thigh of Granite – and thew – of Steel –
Heedless – alike – of pomp – or parting

Ah, Teneriffe!
I'm kneeling – still –

Louise Labé

I LIVE, I DIE, I BURN, I DROWN

I live, I die, I burn, I drown
I endure at once chill and cold
Life is at once too soft and too hard
I have sore troubles mingled with joys

Suddenly I laugh and at the same time cry
And in pleasure many a grief endure
My happiness wanes and yet it lasts unchanged
All at once I dry up and grow green

Thus I suffer love's inconstancies
And when I think the pain is most intense
Without thinking, it is gone again.

Then when I feel my joy is certain
And my hour of greatest delight arrived
I find my pain beginning all over once again.

Translated by Helen R. Lane

Elizabeth I

ON MONSIEUR'S DEPARTURE

I grieve and dare not show my discontent,
I love and yet am forced to seem to hate,
I do, yet dare not say I ever meant,
I seem stark mute but inwardly do prate.
   I am and not, I freeze and yet am burned,
   Since from myself another self I turned.

My care is like my shadow in the sun,
Follows me flying, flies when I pursue it,
Stands and lies by me, doth what I have done.
His too familiar care doth make me rue it.
   No means I find to rid him from my breast,
   Till by the end of things it be supprest.

Some gentler passion slide into my mind,
For I am soft and made of melting snow;
Or be more cruel, love, and so be kind.
Let me or float or sink, be high or low.
   Or let me live with some more sweet content.
   Or die and so forget what love ere meant.

Anne Finch, Countess of Winchilsea

THE UNEQUAL FETTERS

Cou'd we stop the time that's flying
   Or recall it when 'tis past
Put far off the day of Dying
   Or make Youth forever last
To Love wou'd then be worth our cost.

But since we must loose those Graces
   Which at first your hearts have wonne
And you seek for in new Faces
   When our Spring of Life is done
It wou'd but urdge our ruine on

Free as Nature's first intention
    Was to make us, I'll be found
Nor by subtle Man's invention
    Yeild to be in Fetters bound
By one that walks a freer round.

Mariage does but slightly tye Men
    Whil'st close Pris'ners we remain
They the larger Slaves of Hymen
    Still are begging Love again
At the full length of all their chain.

Huang O

TO THE TUNE 'RED EMBROIDERED SHOES'

If you don't know how, why pretend?
Maybe you can fool some girls,
But you can't fool Heaven.
I dreamed you'd play with the
Locust blossom under my green jacket,
Like a eunuch with a courtesan.
But lo and behold
All you can do is mumble.
You've made me all wet and slippery,
But no matter how hard you try
Nothing happens. So stop.
Go and make somebody else
Unsatisfied.

Translated by Kenneth Rexroth and Ling Chun

Hwang-Chin-i

I CUT IN TWO

I cut in two
A long November night, and
Place half under the coverlet,
Sweet-scented as a spring breeze.
And when he comes, I shall take it out,
Unroll it inch by inch, to stretch the night.

Translated by Peter Lee

Helene Cixous

From VIVRE L'ORANGE

In urgency, I begged. *Give me your dish*, I said, icy
words in my mouth. Eat cabbage soup to try to warm
up? Little cabbage lamellae cut up into little pieces in a
dish that gets cold very quickly, to try to save the soul? I
looked at the pieces, very closely, I tried to recall.
What's the use? A woman needs women in order to live.
My outer soul was completely frozen. Cold is the curse!
A woman needs the warm touch. To give warmth. A
soup does not hold the warmth. We need to love, love.
We cannot live without the presence of women who pay
attention to life. '*It is not the soup that will save me,* I said.
*Give me your warmth, the burning warm of your body, it's
that one I need to not die of cold. I need living warmth.*' We
cannot appease our hunger with dishes of soup, we
cannot warm our souls by eating. To secure life we need
to feel that women are living nigh to us.

Clarice is the name of a woman capable of calling life
by all of its warm and cool names. And life comes. She
says *I am*. And in the instant Clarice is. Clarice is
entirely in the instant when she gives herself to being,
alive, infinite, unlimited in her being. When I say:
Clarice, it is not simply to speak to you of a person, it is
to call Clarice a joy, – a fear, – a frightened joy. To tell
you this joy, give you this fear, this joy in a fear.

– To know who is the joy, where, to know her
non-face, her features strikingly mobile, almost
immobile. Fear of joy?

To have the fortune – little sister of joy – to have
encountered the joy clarice, or the joy g h or l or anna,
and since then to live *in* joy, in her infinitely great arms,
her cosmic arms, dry and warm, tender, slim – The too
great fortune? –

to be in her arms, she holds me, being in her space,
for days and days, and summer nights, and since then,
to live, a little above myself, in a fever, a suspension, an
inner race.
– as if I were fleeing her? But I am not really fleeing
her; as if I were putting her to the test, as if I were only
clearing the space in front of me for a new call, so that
she might call me, as if I was calling her, not because she
is no longer there, but so that she might come and
come, and come again a first time,
as a woman makes love, in love, yet, nights and days,
in flight, to be in her arms as if I wanted to measure her,
test her, with an oblivion. But forgetfulness also carries
me away, to the other side of the world, towards her.

Translated by Anne Liddle and Sarah Cornell

Sulpicia

LIGHT OF MY LIFE

Light of my life, let me not be so burning a concern to you
    as I seemed to have been a few days ago,
If in my whole youth I in my folly have ever done anything
    which I admit to have been more sorry for
Than last night, when I left you alone,
Wanting to hide my passion.

Translated by Jane McIntosh Snyder

Alexis de Veaux

THE SISTERS

Ntabuu
Ntabuu   Selina and
Ntabuu of the red dirt road in New Orleans. Red dirt morning.
Hang dry sun below restless maple trees.

>   truckload of farm workermen
>   Come juggle down the road
>   a hundred faces closed   in the dawn
>   move along, move along . . .

In a home made wooden love seat Selina moves nearer. Ntabuu feels
the warm hip and white gabardine skirt close. Selina blows
cigarette ash from her bare breasts rising and falling voluptuous black.
Ntabuu
Ntabuu
Selina
Ntabuu is 27. She two months baby swollen. Mozambique skin purple
she gapped tooth with nigger-toe eyes. Her squat body full of
future unknown/her face solid woman stone. Yellow linen skirt folds
pleat her thigh. In summer hot like this she does not wear panties
she rather her touch-garden sweat (than itch) in July.

>   farm workerman sing along
>   sing along . . .

'You love him?
'No.'
'You want to marry him?'
'No.'
'Why you having this baby?'
'Because we can't make one of our own.'

Selina she 33 years old. Her charcoal body is angular and firm.
She has never had a child or a man. She has never wanted one.
She has always wanted to sing and decorate houses. Always loved
her big white teeth and sculptured lips inherited from their
grandmother.

'Just cause I want a baby Selina don't mean I love you any less.'
'What *do* it mean?'
'God is̄ moving in me Selina. This is God.'
'Bullshit.'

> . . .a hundred faces closed in the migratory
> dawn
> lips dream last night's kisses
> bronze
> move along, sing along . . .

Ntabuu
Ntabuu
Ntabuu the pregnant dancer. Do splits for Selina. Do one two
three kick. One two up. Kick. One two three down. Kick split
for Selina in the next room singing do–rc–mi–fa–so–la 3 days
a week when students come see their 16 room Southern palace.
Inherited from a half French grandmother. Knic knacs traditions
and crystal tables. Old photographs of old aunts and great uncles
in big hats and 2-tone shoes.

'What time is the doctor coming?'
'8:00 or soon after he said.'
'You could still change your mind.'
'No.'
'Why goddamnit? We don't need nobody else.'
'We got to have an heir.'

In the evenings when the townmen come back sun tired/smelling
of fruit trees and oppression they come see the Sisters. Come
bring them berry apple pear and Selina cigarettes. Selina did not
know one night one month someone slept over.

> Ntabuu give good massages he tells the others
> wait their turn their back muscles ache
> for her dancing touch maybe
> ache for the caress
> of julep oil heated on the wood burning stove . . .

'Ntabuu you love me?'
'Yes Selina.'
'You mine?'
'Yes but you can't own me.'

Ntabuu
Ntabuu love her sister/Selina.
Ntabuu
Ntabuu

'You love me Selina?'
'Yes girl.'
'You want to marry me?'
'You crazy.'
'Marry me Selina.'
'I marry you.'
'Do it proper.'

Do it voluptuous mornings like this one. In their 4-posted bed.
Ntabuu rolls closer. Musk oil and lapis lazuli. Her small hand
explores nipple. Selina purrs. Ntabuu fondles the sassy blackness
breathing beneath her own. Tongue and tender. Fingers trail her
stomach quivers. Ntabuu. Open. Selina. Ntabuu. Way down. Purr
Selina.

Purr, Open way down. Slow chant for Isis and Nefertiti.
Probe her royal magic. Smell the bold journey. Wait. Flutter.
Pulse Ntabuu. Cling Selina. Tangle fingers in hair and slow love
sweat. Ancient graffiti hidden on vulva walls.

Princess Zeb-un-Nissa

THOUGH I AM LAILA OF THE PERSIAN ROMANCE

Though I am Laila of the Persian romance,
my heart loves like ferocious Majnun.
I want to go to the desert
but modesty is chains on my feet.
A nightingale came to the flower garden
because she was my pupil.
I am an expert in things of love.
Even the moth is my disciple.

Translated by Willis Barnstone

Patrizia Vicinelli

JADE, OR THE MEDEA WITHIN US

Jade, or the Medea within us.
For such to exploit the cedars of your mind, the tiny doll found
shattered, which lapidary level of my thought do you work in, a
discovery forever thaumaturgical.
On the day of the tragedy red-hot burns me, although an agnostic
rebellious unshorn hammock, but this cradle of night that eagerly
soiled the cries revolved, and already it was over in the dip of
black blood infusing any work you choose.
Regally the house of death approaches, oblong vicissitudes,
crooked lanes and prevailing sadness – but for one violet light.
What threatens? Perhaps a madness of days, or a lost merry night
my senses overwhelmed by usura, sharp insatiables postponed in a
sweet poison, call it farewell, when density and remaining time
fade away.
Murdered on the rope to the Etruscan, subtle anamnesis of a
procession smooth as a viper, a beautiful glittering skin causing
no feeling from without, opaque usura.
Thoughtless atavistic luxury   an empire is an empire she cried
and spots of blood like panties dampened early, so early, heard
her between screams, a sense of desperation long modelled in your
bonny-baby eyelashes.
How badly they had reduced her baking-tin and casket, a thousand
swampy lies under the pretext of being king.
How did you want to live? Your temple within a poisonous crystal
oasis, how brave we are to give time all its security.
In her passion she smiles red   the banner comes to an end and
meanwhile children scream, dark winter howls choke in the completed
act.   Indifferent, she takes no part in the mourning.

Translated by Franco Beltramettii and Tom Raworth

Solveig Von Schoultz

THE LOVER

My eyes want to kiss your face.
I have no power over my eyes.
They just want to kiss your face.
I flow towards you out of my eyes,
a fine heat trembles round your shoulders,
it slowly dissolves your contours
and I am there with you, your mouth
and everywhere around you –
I have no power over my eyes.

I sit with my hands in my lap,
I shan't touch you and I'll never speak.
But my eyes kiss your face,
I rise out of myself and no-one can stop me,
I flow out and I'm invisible,
I cannot stop this unfathomable flowing,
this dazzle that knows neither end nor beginning –
but when at last you turn your eyes towards me,
your unaware, questioning, stranger's eyes,
I sink myself back into my hands
and take up my place again under my eyelids.

Translated by Anne Born

Aphra Behn

THE DISAPPOINTMENT

I

One day the amorous *Lysander*,
By an impatient Passion sway'd,
Surpriz'd fair *Cloris*, that lov'd Maid,
Who could defend her self no longer.
All things did with his Love conspire;
The gilded Planet of the Day,
In his gay Chariot drawn by Fire,
Was now descending to the Sea,
And left no Light to guide the World,
But what from *Cloris* Brighter Eyes was hurld.

II

In a Lone Thicket made for Love,
Silent as yielding Maids Consent,
She with a Charming Languishment,
Permits his Force, yet gently strove;
Her hands his Bosom softly meet,
But not to put him back design'd,
Rather to draw 'em on inclin'd:
Whilst he lay trembling at her Feet,
Resistance 'tis in vain to show;
She wants the pow'r to say – *Ah! What d'ye do?*

III

Her Bright Eyes sweet, and yet severe,
Where Love and Shame confus'dly strive.
Fresh Vigor to *Lysander* give;
And breathing faintly in his Ear,
She cry'd – *Cease, Cease – your vain Desire,*
Or I'll call out – What would you do?
My Dearer Honour ev'n to You
I cannot, must not give – Retire,
Or take this Life, whose chiefest part
I gave you with the Conquest of my Heart.

IV

But he as much unus'd to Fear,
As he was capable of Love,
The blessed minutes to improve,
Kisses her Mouth, her Neck, her Hair;
Each Touch her new Desire Alarms,
His burning trembling Hand he prest
Upon her swelling Snowy Brest,
While she lay panting in his Arms.
All her Unguarded Beauties lie
The Spoils and Trophies of the Enemy.

V

And now without Respect or Fear,
He seeks the Object of his Vows,
(His Love no Modesty allows)
By swift degrees advancing – where
His daring Hand that Altar seiz'd,
Where Gods of Love do sacrifice:
That Awful Throne, that Paradice
Where Rage is calm'd, and Anger pleas'd;
That fountain where Delight still flows,
And gives the Universal World Repose.

VI

Her Balmy Lips incountring his,
Their Bodies, as their Souls, are joyn'd;
Where both in Transports Unconfin'd
Extend themselves upon the Moss.
Cloris half dead and breathless lay;
Her soft Eyes cast a Humid Light,
Such as divides the Day and Night;
Or falling Stars, whose Fires decay:
And now no signs of Life she shows,
But what in short-breath'd Sighs returns and goes.

VII

He saw how at her Length she lay;
He saw her rising Bosom bare;
Her loose thin *Robes*, through which appear
A Shape design'd for Love and Play;
Abandon'd by her Pride and Shame.
She does her softest Joys dispence,
Off'ring her Virgin-Innocence
A Victim to Loves Sacred Flame;
While the o'er-Ravish'd Shepherd lies
Unable to perform the Sacrifice.

VIII

Ready to taste a thousand Joys,
The too transported hapless Swain
Found the vast Pleasure turn'd to Pain;
Pleasure which too much Love destroys:
The willing Garments by he laid,
And Heaven all open'd to his view,
Mad to possess, himself he threw
On the Defenceless Lovely Maid.
But Oh what envying God conspires
To snatch his Power, yet leave him the Desire!

IX

Nature's Support, (without whose Aid
She can no Humane Being give)
It self now wants the Art to live;
Faintness its slack'ned Nerves invade:
In vain th' inraged Youth essay'd
To call its fleeting Vigor back.
No motion 'twill from Motion take;
Excess of Love his Love betray'd:
In vain he Toils, in vain Commands;
The Insensible fell weeping in his Hand.

X

In this so Amorous Cruel Strife,
Where Love and Fate were too severe,
The poor *Lysander* in despair
Renounc'd his Reason with his Life:
Now all the brisk and active Fire
That should the Nobler Part inflame,
Serv'd to increase his Rage and Shame,
And left no Spark for New Desire:
Not all her Naked Charms cou'd move
Or calm that Rage that had debauch'd his Love.

XI

Cloris returning from the Trance
Which Love and soft Desire had bred,
Her timerous Hand she gently laid
(Or guided by Design or Chance)
Upon that Fabulous *Priapus*,
That Potent God, as Poets feign;
But never did young *Shepherdess*,
Gath'ring of Fern upon the Plain,
More nimbly draw her Fingers back,
Finding beneath the verdant Leaves a Snake:

XII

Than *Cloris* her fair Hand withdrew,
Finding that God of her Desires
Disarm'd of all his Awful Fires,
And Cold as Flow'rs bath'd in the Morning Dew.
Who can the *Nymph's* Confusion guess?
The Blood forsook the hinder Place,
And strew'd with Blushes all her Face,
Which both Disdain and Shame exprest:
And from *Lysander's* Arms she fled,
Leaving him fainting on the Gloomy Bed.

XIII

Like Lightning through the Grove she hies,
Or *Daphne* from the *Delphick God*,
No Print upon the grassey Road
She leaves, t' instruct Pursuing Eyes.
The Wind that wanton'd in her Hair,
And with her Ruffled Garments plaid,
Discover'd in the Flying Maid
All that the Gods e'er made, if Fair.
So *Venus*, when her *Love* was slain,
With Fear and Haste flew o'er the Fatal Plain.

XIV

The *Nymph's* Resentments none but I
Can well Imagine or Condole:
But none can guess *Lysander's* Soul,
But those who sway'd his Destiny.
His silent Griefs swell up to Storms,
And not one God his Fury spares;
He curs'd his Birth, his Fate, his Stars;
But more the *Shepherdess's* Charms,
Whose soft bewitching Influence
Had damn'd him to the *Hell* of Impotence.

Katherine Philips

AN ANSWER TO ANOTHER PERSUADING A LADY TO MARRIAGE

FORBEAR, bold youth, all's Heaven here,
    And what you do aver,
To others, courtship may appear,
    'Tis sacriledge to her.

She is a publick deity,
    And were't not very odd
She should depose her self to be
    A petty household god?

First make the sun in private shine,
   And bid the world adieu,
That so he may his beams confine
   In complement to you.

But if of that you do despair,
   Think how you did amiss,
To strive to fix her beams which are
   More bright and large than this.

Susan Ludvigson

PARIS AUBADE

Breathing, the last possession
that counts, comes faster here, where
time and our oldest obsessions

make us more conscious – self-conscious. The air
is completely polluted, of course, but haze
that descends on this city is like the fair

skin of Doris Day, filmed in the days
when soft light meant dropping gauze
in front of the camera. It's like that these lazy

first weeks when we stay in bed until noon, lawless
as coupling cats we hear on the balcony, late.
We inhale each morning as if the flawed

fabric of earlier lives had been laid
in a drawer, carefully folded, forever.
Yet under the net of that dream, we pay

for what we know. Bodies that flail under covers
all hours in pleasure learn to count breaths –
just after. Though the world falls away for lovers

as they make the escape into flesh,
its heavy atmosphere fills them. Clouds
are the color of nipples. Worn silk thins to mesh.

Marina Tsvetaeva

WHERE DOES THIS TENDERNESS COME FROM?

Where does this tenderness come from?
These are not the – first curls I
have stroked slowly – and lips I
have known are – darker than yours

as stars rise often and go out again
(where does this tenderness come from?)
so many eyes have risen and died out
   in front of these eyes of mine.

and yet no such song have
I heard in the darkness of night before,
(where does this tenderness come from?):
   here, on the ribs of the singer.

Where does this tenderness come from?
And what shall I do with it, young
sly singer, just passing by?
Your lashes are – longer than anyone's.

Translated by Elaine Feinstein

Nina Cassian

PRAYER

If you really exist – show up
as a bear, a goat, a pilot,
come with eyes, mouth, voice,
– demand something from me,
force me to sacrifice myself,
take me in your arms, protect me from above,
feed me with the seventh part of one fish,
hiss at me, reanimate my fingers,
refill me with aromas, with astonishment
– resurrect me.

Translated by Brenda Walker
and Andrea Deletant

Ephelia

TO ONE THAT ASKED ME WHY I LOVED J.G.

Why do I love? go ask the glorious sun
Why every day it round the world doth run:
Ask Thames and Tiber why they ebb and flow:
Ask damask roses why in June they blow:
Ask ice and hail the reason why they're cold:
Decaying beauties, why they will grow old:
They'll tell thee, Fate, that everything doth move,
Inforces them to this, and me to love.
There is no reason for our love or hate,
'Tis irresistible as Death or Fate;
'Tis not his face; I've sense enough to see,
That is not good, though doated on by me:
Nor is't his tongue, that has this conquest won,
For that at least is equalled by my own:
His carriage can to none obliging be,
'Tis rude, affected, full of vanity:
Strangely ill natur'd, peevish and unkind,
Unconstant, false, to jealousy inclin'd:
His temper could not have so great a power,
'Tis mutable, and changes every hour:
Those vigorous years that women so adore
Are past in him: he's twice my age and more;
And yet I love this false, this worthless man,
With all the passion that a woman can;
Doat on his imperfections, though I spy
Nothing to love; I love, and know not why.
Since 'tis decreed in the dark book of Fate,
That I should love, and he should be ingrate.

Carolyn Kizer

WHAT THE BONES KNOW

Remembering the past
And gloating at it now,
I know the frozen brow
And shaking sides of lust
Will dog me at my death
To catch my ghostly breath..

I think that Yeats was right,
That lust and love are one.
The body of this night
May beggar me to death,
But we are not undone
Who love with all our breath.

I know that Proust was wrong,
His wheeze: love, to survive,
Needs jealousy, and death
And lust, to make it strong
Or goose it back alive.
Proust took away my breath.

The later Yeats was right
To think of sex and death
And nothing else. Why wait
Till we are turning old?
My thoughts are hot and cold.
I do not waste my breath.

Edith Södergran

WHAT IS TOMORROW?

What is tomorrow? Perhaps not you.
Perhaps another's arms and a new contact and a similar pain . . .
I shall leave you with a certainty like no other:
I shall come back as a fragment of your own pain.
I shall come to you from another sky with a new resolve.

I shall come to you from another star with the same look.
I shall come to you with my old longing in new features.
I shall come to you strange, angry and faithful
with the footfalls of a wild beast out of your heart's far desert
      homeland.
You will fight against me hard and powerlessly
as one only fights against one's destiny, against one's luck,
      against one's star.
I shall smile and bind silken threads around my finger
and I shall hide the little spool of your destiny in the folds of
      my clothes.

Translated by David McDuff

Wu Tsao

FOR THE COURTESAN CH'ING LIN

To the tune 'The Love of the Immortals'

On your slender body
Your jade and coral girdle ornaments chime
Like those of a celestial companion
Come from the Green Jade City of Heaven.
One smile from you when we meet,
And I become speechless and forget every word.
For too long you have gathered flowers,
And leaned against the bamboos,
Your green sleeves growing cold,
In your deserted valley:
I can visualize you all alone,
A girl harboring her cryptic thoughts.

You glow like a perfumed lamp
In the gathering shadows.
We play wine games
And recite each other's poems.
Then you sing 'Remembering South of the River'
With its heart breaking verses. Then
We paint each other's beautiful eyebrows.

I want to possess you completely –
Your jade body
And your promised heart.
It is Spring.
Vast mists cover the Five Lakes.
My dear, let me buy a red painted boat
And carry you away.

Translated by Kenneth Rexroth

Shushanig Gourghenian

DESIRE

I wanted to welcome you
into my soul like a god,
lost and road weary
to hear you calling this
    home.

I wanted to restrict
the nightingale to but one
garden. And keep his free
songs for me
    alone.

I wanted you jailed
in my breast as part
of the flow of my blood,
the sway of my
    bones.

I wanted when I died
my name to be carved
on that hardest of monuments
your heart of
    stone.

Translated by
Diana Der Hovanessian

H.D. [Hilda Doolittle]

FRAGMENT THIRTY-SIX

I know not what to do:
my mind is divided – Sappho.

I know not what to do,
my mind is reft:
is song's gift best?
is love's gift loveliest?
I know not what to do,
now sleep has pressed
weight on your eyelids.

Shall I break your rest,
devouring, eager?
Is love's gift best?
nay, song's the loveliest:
yet were you lost,
what rapture
could I take from song?
what song were left?

I know not what to do:
to turn and slake
the rage that burns,
with my breath burn
and trouble your cool breath?
so shall I turn and take
snow in my arms?
(is love's gift best?)
yet flake on flake
of snow were comfortless,
did you lie wondering,
wakened yet unawake.

Shall I turn and take
comfortless snow within my arms?
press lips to lips

that answer not,
press lips to flesh
that shudders not nor breaks?

Is love's gift best?
shall I turn and slake
all the wild longing?
O I am eager for you!
as the Pleiads shake
white light in whiter water
so shall I take you?

My mind is quite divided,
my minds hesitate,
so perfect matched,
I know not what to do:
each strives with each
as two white wrestlers
standing for a match,
ready to turn and clutch
yet never shake muscle nor nerve nor tendon;
so my mind waits
to grapple with my mind,
yet I lie quiet,
I would seem at rest.

I know not what to do:
strain upon strain,
sound surging upon sound
makes my brain blind;
as a wave-line may wait to fall
yet (waiting for its falling)
still the wind may take
from off its crest,
white flake on flake of foam,
that rises,
seeming to dart and pulse
and rend the light,
so my mind hesitates
above the passion
quivering yet to break,

so my mind hesitates
above my mind,
listening to song's delight.

I know not what to do:
will the sound break,
rending the night
with rift on rift of rose
and scattered light?
Will the sound break at last
as the wave hesitant,
or will the whole night pass
and I lie listening awake?

Helen Kidd

MEANWHILE CESARIO DANCING

i

whistling on the inside of your breath   and I know well
this trick   a secret music's edge   and although
you've said   'but unsuspend your disbelief'
seeing you then out there   that long sun-sweep across
you face   friend   air on my side   a flock of star-
lings in my head   hands in their pockets   and that

foiled and sheeny whale of a travelling sun inside the tree-
arms' fish-net trails   (or might have been);   and it's as if
among their dancing arcs and casts   it pretends it can
explain away to me my own particular and out-of-focus way
of looking out too far.

ii

and seeing you still out there beyond the wall and glass
of bookish silence that can drown

                                        unless you now should lean out
to open it towards   and listen where this rushing past us
comes   unloosen you ears' intent and inward-turned attention.

so seeing you again   this whispering's Rapunzel down
a trace of ruined casements   (may have been)   or as if
the lifting of a head towards its air asks . . .
'Or who has lipped so easily between the first befores of knowing
it   its for-hints paler than the light advance of paws ?'
unless the silver of itself could catch the comb of air
along its greening points of early spring tact

for no-one else could

iii

seeing you there then and your dreams' freedoms hatching
patterns where condensed drops have defined the glass
were once my breath of words   so this remains as simple
as the lost action of refracting secondary light   as
a fresnel might catch   en-courant   a shadow of
not so much the action of the hand   as of the arm
not so much the whole arm   as of the movement from the heart.

Sappho

HE IS MORE THAN A HERO

He is more than a hero

He is a god in my eyes –
the man who is allowed
to sit beside you – he

who listens intimately
to the sweet murmur of
your voice, the enticing

laughter that makes my own
heart beat fast. If I meet
you suddenly, I can't

speak – my tongue is broken;
a thin flame runs under
my skin; seeing nothing,

hearing only my own ears
drumming, I drip with sweat;
trembling shakes my body

and I turn paler than
dry grass. At such times
death isn't far from me

Translated by Mary Barnard

Lady Grisel Baillie

WERENA MY HEART'S LICHT

There ance was a may, and she lo'ed na men;
She biggit her bonnie bow'r doun in yon glen;
But now she cries, Dool, and a well-a-day!
Come doun the green gait and come here away!

When bonnie young Johnnie cam owre the sea,
He said he saw naething sae lovely as me;
He hecht me baith rings and mony braw things –
And werena my heart's licht, I wad dee.

He had a wee titty that loe'd na me,
Because I was twice as bonny as she;
She raised sic a pother 'twixt him and his mother
That werena my heart's licht, I wad dee.

The day it was set, and the bridal to be:
The wife took a dwam and lay doun to dee;
She maned and she graned out o' dolour and pain,
Till he vow'd he never wad see me again.

His kin was for ane of a higher degree,
Said – What had he do wi' the likes of me?
Appose I was bonnie, I wasna for Johnnie –
And werena my heart's licht, I wad dee.

They said I had neither cow nor calf,
Nor dribbles o' drink ring through the draff,
Nor pickles o' meal rins thro' the mill e'e–
And werena my heart's licht, I wad dee.

His titty she was baith wylie and slee:
She spied me as I cam owre the lea;
And then she ran in, and made a loud din –
Believe your ain e'en, and ye trow not me.

His bonnet stood ay fu' round on his brow,
His auld ane look'd ay as well as some's new
But now he lets't wear ony gait it will hing,
And casts himself dowie upon the corn bing.

And now he gaes daund'ring about the dykes,
And a' he dow do is to hund the tykes:
The live-lang nicht he ne'er steeks his e'e –
And werena my heart's licht, I wad dee.

Were I but young for thee, as I hae been,
We should hae been gallopin' doun on yon green,
And linkin' it owre the lily-white lea –
And wow, gin I were but young for thee!

Gloria Fuertes

WHEN I HEAR YOUR NAME

When I hear your name
I feel a little robbed of it;
it seems unbelievable
that half a dozen letters could say so much.

My compulsion is to blast down every wall with your name,
I'd paint it on all the houses,
there wouldn't be a well
I hadn't leaned into
to shout your name there,
nor a stone mountain
where I hadn't uttered
those six separate letters
that are echoed back.

My compulsion is
to teach the birds to sing it,
to teach the fish to drink it,
to teach men that there is nothing
like the madness of repeating your name.

My compulsion is to forget altogether
the other 22 letters, all the numbers,
the books I've read, the poems I've written.
To say hello with your name.
To beg bread with your name.
'She always says the same thing,' they'd say when they saw me,
and I'd be so proud, so happy, so self-contained.

And I'll go to the other world with your name on my tongue,
and all their questions I'll answer with your name
– the judges and saints will understand nothing –
God will sentence me to repeating it endlessly and forever.

Translated by Philip Levine and Ada Long

Jayne Cortez

ROSE SOLITUDE

For Duke Ellington

I am essence of Rose Solitude
my cheeks are laced with cognac
my hips sealed with five satin nails
i carry dreams and romance of new fools and old flames
between the musk of fat
and the side pocket of my mink tongue

Listen to champagne bubble from this solo

Essence of Rose Solitude
veteran from texas   tiger from chicago   that's me
i cover the shrine of Duke
who like Satchmo   like Nat (King) Cole
will never die because love they say
never dies

I tell you from stair steps of these navy blue nights
these metallic snakes
these flashing fish skins
and the melodious cry of Shango
surrounded by sorrow
by purple velvet tears
by cockhounds limping from crosses
from turtle skinned shoes
from diamond shaped skulls and canes
made from dead gazelles
wearing a face of wilting potato plants
of grey and black scissors
of bee bee shots and fifty red boils
yes the whole world loved him

I tell you from suspenders of two-timing dog odors
from inca frosted lips
nonchalant legs
i tell you from howling chant of sister Erzulie
and the exaggerated hearts of a hundred pretty
women
they loved him
this world sliding from a single flower
into a caravan of heads made into ten thousand
flowers

Ask me
Essence of Rose Solitude
chickadee from arkansas that's me
i sleep on cotton bones
cotton tails
and mellow myself in empty ballrooms
i'm no fly by night
look at my resume
i walk through the eyes of staring lizards
i throw my neck back to floorshow on bumping goat skins
in front of my stage fright
i cover the hands of Duke who like Satchmo
like Nat (King) Cole will never die
because love they say
never dies

Janet Sutherland

TO THE SPIDER IN THE CREVICE/
BEHIND THE TOILET DOOR

i have left you four flies
three are in the freezer next to the joint of beef
the other is wrapped in christmas paper
tied with a pink ribbon
beside the ironing table in the hall
should you need to contact me
in an emergency
the number's in the book
by the telephone.

p.s. i love you

Eunice de Souza

ALIBI

My love says
for god's sake
don't write poems
which heave and pant
and resound to the music
of our thighs
etc.
Just keep at what you are:
a sour old puss in verse
and leave the rest to me.

Sarah Kirsch

THE INCANTATION

Phoebus red crashing wall of cloud
Swim under his lid mingle
With my hair
Tie him tight so he can't tell
Whether it's Monday or Friday or

What century it is whether he's
Read Ovid or seen him whether I
Am his spoon his wife or
Just some cloud creature
Athwart the sky

Translated by Anthony Vivis

Dorothy Parker

CHANT FOR DARK HOURS

Some men, some men
Cannot pass a
Book shop.
(Lady, make your mind up, and wait your life away.)

Some men, some men
Cannot pass a
Crap game.
(He said he'd come at moonrise, and here's another day!)

Some men, some men
Cannot pass a
Bar-room.
(Wait about, and hang about, and that's the way it goes.)

Some men, some men
Cannot pass a
Woman.
(Heaven never send me another one of those!)

Some men, some men
Cannot pass a
Golf course.
(Read a book, and sew a seam, and slumber if you can.)

Some men, some men
Cannot pass a
Haberdasher's.
(All your life you wait around for some damn man!)

Emily Dickinson

I SEE THEE BETTER – IN THE DARK

I see thee better – in the Dark –
I do not need a Light –
The Love of Thee – a Prism be –
Excelling Violet –

I see thee better for the Years
That hunch themselves between –
The Miner's Lamp – sufficient be –
To nullify the Mine –

And in the Grave – I see Thee best –
Its little Panels be
Aglow – All ruddy – with the Light
I held so high, for Thee –

What need of Day –
To those whose Dark – hath so – surpassing Sun –
It deem it be – Continually –
At the Meridian?

Anne Spencer

LINES TO A NASTURTIUM

Flame-flower, Day-torch, Mauna Loa,
I saw a daring bee, today, pause, and soar,
    Into your flaming heart;
Then did I hear crisp crinkled laughter
As the furies after tore him apart?
    A bird, next, small and humming,
Looked into your startled depths and fled . . .
Surely, some dread sight, and dafter
    Than human eyes as mine can see,
Set the stricken air waves drumming
    In his flight.

Day-torch, Flame-flower, cool-hot Beauty,
I cannot see, I cannot hear your fluty
Voice lure your loving swain,
But I know one other to whom you are in beauty
Born in vain;
Hair like the setting sun,
Her eyes a rising star,
Motions gracious as reeds by Babylon, bar
All your competing;
Hands like, how like, brown lilies sweet,
Cloth of gold were fair enough to touch her feet . . .
Ah, how the senses flood at my repeating,
As once in her fire-lit heart I felt the furies
Beating, beating.

Gwendolyn Bennett

TO A DARK GIRL

I love you for your brownness,
And the rounded darkness of your breast,
I love you for the breaking sadness in your voice
And shadows where your wayward eyelids rest.

Something of old forgotten queens
Lurks in the lithe abandon of your walk
And something of the shackled slave
Sobs in the rhythm of your talk.

Oh, little brown girl, born for sorrow's mate,
Keep all you have of queenliness,
Forgetting that you once were slave,
And let your full lips laugh at Fate!

Lady Caroline Nairne

WILL YE NO COME BACK AGAIN?

Bonnie Charlie's now awa',
    Safely owre the friendly main;
Mony a heart will break in twa,
    Should he ne'er come back again.

    Will ye no come back again?
    Will ye no come back again?
    Better lo'ed ye canna be,
    Will ye no come back again?

Ye trusted in your Hieland men,
    They trusted you, dear Charlie;
They kent you hiding in the glen,
    Your cleadin' was but barely.

    Will ye no come back again?
    Will ye no come back again?
    Better lo'ed ye canna be,
    Will ye no come back again?

English bribes were a' in vain,
    An' e'en tho' puirer we may be;
Siller canna buy the heart
    That beats aye for thine and thee.

    Will ye no come back again?
    Will ye no come back again?
    Better lo'ed ye canna be,
    Will ye no come back again?

We watched thee in the gloamin' hour,
    We watched thee in the mornin' grey;
Tho' thirty thousand pounds they'd gi'e,
    Oh there was nane that wad betray.

Will ye no come back again?
Will ye no come back again?
Better lo'ed ye canna be,
Will ye no come back again?

Sweet's the laverock's note and lang,
    Lilting wildly up the glen;
But aye to me he sings ae sang, –
    Will ye no come back again?

Will ye no come back again?
Will ye no come back again?
Better lo'ed ye canna be,
Will ye no come back again?

Caroline Norton

SONNET VI

Where the red wine-cup floweth, there art thou!
Where luxury curtains out the evening sky; –
Triumphant Mirth sits flush'd upon thy brow,
And ready laughter lurks within thine eye.
Where the long day declineth, lone I sit,
In idle thought, my listless hands entwined,
And, faintly smiling at remember'd wit,
Act the scene over to my musing mind.
In my lone dreams I hear thy eloquent voice,
I see the pleased attention of the throng,
And bid my spirit in thy joy rejoice,
Lest in love's selfishness I do thee wrong.
Ah! midst that proud and mirthful company
Send'st *thou* no wondering thought to love and me?

Katherine Philips

TO MY EXCELLENT LUCASIA, ON OUR FRIENDSHIP

I did not live until this time
   Crown'd my felicity,
When I could say without a crime,
   I am not thine, but thee.

This carcass breath'd, and walkt, and slept,
   So that the world believ'd
There was a soul the motions kept;
   But they were all deceiv'd.

For as a watch by art is wound
   To motion, such was mine:
But never had Orinda found
   A soul till she found thine;

Which now inspires, cures and supplies,
   And guides my darkned breast:
For thou art all that I can prize,
   My joy, my life, my rest.

No bridegroom's nor crown-conqueror's mirth
   To mine compar'd can be:
They have but pieces of the earth,
   I've all the world in thee.

Then let our flames still light and shine,
   And no false fear controul,
As innocent as our design,
   Immortal as our soul.

Margaret, Duchess of Newcastle

LOVE AND POETRY

O LOVE, how thou art tired out with rhyme!
Thou art a tree whereon all poets clime;
And from thy branches every one takes some
Of thy sweet fruit, which Fancy feeds upon.
But now thy tree is left so bare and poor,
That they can scarcely gather one plumb more.

Biographical Notes

Valentine Ackland (1906–69) British
Author of more than 2000 poems, most of them unpublished. Variously a Catholic, Communist Party member and Quaker, she was briefly married but lived with Sylvia Townsend Warner for over 30 years in Dorset. They went to Spain together in the Civil War, and worked for the Communist Party in England. She wrote a book on agricultural conditions.

Sonja Åkesson (1926–77) Swedish
Was part of the 1960s 'New Simplicity' movement. Worked variously as salesperson, clerk, housekeeper, etc. Her second marriage to the concrete poet Jarl Hammarberg resulted in several collaboratons. Her *Husfrid* (1963) attracted wide attention for its depiction of the life of a woman in Sweden. Her poetry dealt with loneliness and poverty, and became increasingly dark in the 1970s.

Anna Akhmatova (1889–1966) Russian
One of the great 20th century Russian poets. Spent most of her life in St Petersburg (later Leningrad) where flowers are still left outside the block in which she lived. Suffered much under Stalin (her son was imprisoned), denounced and expelled from the Writers' Union, she was 'rehabilitated' under Khrushchev, and widely recognised by the time of her death.

Gillian Allnutt, British
One of the editors of *Writing Women*, former poetry editor of *City Limits*, now lives and teaches creative writing in Newcastle. Her books include *Spitting the Pips Out* (1981) and *Beginning the Avocado* (1987).

Julia Alvarez, American
Originally from the Dominican Republic, she now lives, teaches and writes in Vermont. *Homecoming* (poems) was published by Grove Press in 1984; forthcoming, a book of short stories, *Daughters of Invention*, from Algonquin, 1991.

Maya Angelou (1928–) American
Autobiographer, poet, performer, director, and teacher. She has written 5 volumes of autobiography, including *I Know Why The Caged Birds Sings*. and 5 volumes of poetry including *And Still I Rise* (1978) and *Sheba Sings the Song* (1987)

Marion Angus (1866–1946) Scottish
A highly influential Lallans (or Lowlands dialect) writer and influence on Hugh McDiarmid.

Ruth Asher-Pettipher, British
A young Rastafarian poet, she lives in Warwickshire and is currently working as a poet with youth groups. She has one pamphlet published, *Reason With a Rhythm* (1990).

Margaret Atwood (1939–) Canadian
Born Ottawa. Leading novelist, poet, critic and short-story writer. Her works include *Survival, The Circle Game, The Animals in that Country, Power Politics, Selected Poems 1966–74*, all poetry, *The Edible Woman, Surfacing, Lady Oracle*, novels. Influential in the discussions on nationalism and nativism, lives on a farm in S. Ontario. *The Handmaid's Tale*, was shortlisted for the Booker Prize. Most recent novel, *Cat's Eye* (1989).

Ingeborg Bachmann (1926–73) Austrian
Studied philosophy and did her doctorate on Heidegger, first poems published 1953. Author of many volumes of prose, poetry, plays and libretti, awarded the Buchner prize 1964 for *Gedichte* (Selected Poetry and Prose).

Elisaveta Bagriana (1893–) Bulgarian
One of the foremost Bulgarian poets, her first book was *Everlasting and Holy* (1927). Later works such as *From Shore to Shore* (1963) show her concern with feminist and political issues.

Lady Grisel Baillie (1665–1746) Scottish
Poet and daybook-keeper. *The Household Book of Lady Grisel Baillie* edited by Scott Moncrieff was published in 1911. 'Werena My Heart's Licht' is her most famous song, it was published in 1726. Eldest of a family of 18, she managed the household affairs, living in exile till 1688. Managed her husband's and father's estates afterwards, and travelled frequently.

Maria Banuş (1914–) Romanian
As well as being a poet, she is a translator, essayist and playwright. First work published in 1928; recent work includes *Anyone and Something* (1972). *Orologiu cu Figuri* (1984). Besides many volumes of her own poetry, she has translated Goethe, Rilke, Browning and Pushkin.

Natalie Barney (1876–1972) American
Lived in Paris from 1902–46, the centre of a salon for women writers whom she encouraged, and where she used her fortune to encourage both social and literary life amongst her protégés. Philosophically, sexually and politically in advance of her time, she published infrequently but wrote in many forms – poetry, drama, gothic fiction, biography, autobiography, pensées and memoirs – largely in French.

Elizabeth Barrett Browning (1806–61) English
A major English poet, she acquired her education from her brothers' tutors. A precocious writer, dedicated to the abolition of slavery and the women's struggle, she shared friendships with leading women of her time (Harriet

Martineau, Margaret Fuller). Author of the blank verse novel *Aurora Leigh*. After her marriage to Robert Browning she lived in Italy.

Aphra Behn (1640–89) English
The first professional woman of letters in England. Bohemian, feminist, anti-Whig, sometime secret agent for King Charles, she was imprisoned for debt. Afterwards wrote 17 plays, several histories and novels, as well as many poems.

Gwendolyn Bennet (1902–81) American
Poet and graphic artist, editor of *Opportunity* magazine during the Harlem Renaissance of the 1920s. Poetry widely anthologised, including in *The Book of American Poetry*, ed. James Weldon Johnson (1922).

Mei-Mei Berssenbrugge (1947–) American
Born in Peking, educated in Columbia, she now lives in New Mexico, Writer and visiting professor. Works include *Fish Souls* (1971), *Summits Move with the Tide* (1974), *Random Possession* –1, (1979), *The Heat Bud* (1982).

Elizabeth Bishop (1911–79) American
Born in Massachusetts, brought up in Nova Scotia, she travelled widely and settled in Brazil. *Complete Poems 1927–79* published 1983.

Eavan Boland (1945–) Irish
Born in Dublin. Lecturer at Trinity College, Dublin. Recent works include: *The Journey* (1987). A volume of *Selected Poems* came out from Carcanet in 1989. Author of *New Territory* (1967), *The War Horse* (1975), *In Her Own Image* (1980).

Lucy Boston (1892–1990) English
Author of many famous children's books, two novels, a volume of autobiography and a book of poetry. Lived near St Ives, Cambridgeshire in a 12th century moated manor house.

Mistress Anne Bradstreet (1612–72) American
Born and grew up in England, sailed for the New World two years after her marriage. Her first book of poems was published in London, 1650 and an authorised edition of her poems was published 1678. Her father and husband were prominent in Massachusetts; she had eight children. She is seen as America's first poet.

Jean Binta Breeze (1957–) Jamaican
Actress and first woman dub poet, lives and works in Brixton. Does performances and recordings and teaches at Brixton College. She is also a playwright with many playscripts to her credit, a dancer and choreographer. Her performances are well known throughout Britain; amongst her books are *Answers* (1983) and *Riddym Ravings & Other Poems* (1988)

Emily Brontë (1818–48) British
One of Britain's finest Romantic poets, she lived most of her life at her father's parsonage in Haworth, Yorkshire apart from eight months in Brussels. She is best known for *Wuthering Heights*, but also wrote many of the Gondal poems, deriving from all the Brontë childrens' world of legend and fantasy.

Gwendolyn Brooks (1917–) American
First African–American to receive the Pulitzer prize in 1950 for *Annie Allen*. Numerous volumes of poetry, including *A Street in Bronzeville* (1945), *In the Mecca* (1968) and the novella *Maud Martha* (1953).

Olga Broumas, American
Teaches on a fine arts programme, is a musician and bodywork therapist and travels widely giving readings and talks. Books include *Black Holes, Black Stockings* (with Jane Miller) and *Selected Translations of Odysseus Elytis*.

Catherine Byron (1947–) English/Irish
She spent her childhood in Belfast and later came to England. Educated at Oxford. Her books include *Settlements* (1985), *Samhain* (1987); work in progress on a feminist reading of Seamus Heaney. Author of *Station Island Journal* (prose) for which she received a Leverhulme award.

Nina Cassian (1924 –) Romanian
Studied drama and painting in Bucharest, she writes books for children and composes music. Has been visiting professor teaching creative writing in New York, and recently in Britain. One of the leading Romanian poets.

Eibhlín Dhubh ní Chonaill (1743–?) Irish
One of 20 children, she eloped with husband Art O'Leary. He was killed by the High Sheriff after a dispute over a horse. Her famous lament has been translated many times, and is very long in its original form.

Hélène Cixous (1937–) French
Lives in Paris. Professor at the University of Paris, founder and director of the centre for women's studies there and in 1969 of the *Revue de Theorie et D'Analyse Littéraire Poètique*. Author of more than 30 works of fiction and essays, and five plays. Her thesis on James Joyce was translated in 1972, and six further works, including *Dedans* (1969), *Angst* (1977), *Livre de Promethea* (1983).

Lucille Clifton (1936–) American
Author of many volumes of poetry, including, *Good News About the Earth* (1972) and *Two-Headed Woman* (1980).

Anne Cluysenaar (1936–) Irish
Daughter of the painter John Cluysenaar. Her *The Double Helix* was published by Carcanet. 'Dark Mothers' is from 'Gilgamesh Variations', a series of poems and paintings set in Wales, as yet unpublished. She recently left

academic life to write and paint full-time, and lives in Wales with her husband, Walter Freeman Jackson.

Norma Cole, Canadian
Lives in San Francisco. Author of *Mace Hill Remap* and *Metamorphopsia*. Her translation of Danielle Collobert's 'Il Donc', as 'It Then' is forthcoming from O Books.

Gillian Clarke (1937–) Welsh
Born and lives in Cardiff. Writer, has been a lecturer in art history, teaches creative writing. Works include *Snow on the Mountain* (1972), *The Sundial* (1978, winner of Welsh Arts Council poetry prize), *Letter From a Far Country* (1982). She is also an editor of *The Anglo-Welsh review*.

Sally Cline (1939–) British
Write and feminist, author of *Just Desserts: Women and Food* (1990) and co-author with Dale Spender of *Reflecting Men at Twice Their Natural Size* (1987) both published by Andre Deutsch. She is working on a book of stories about women's violent and faithful lives.

La Comtesse de Dia (born *c*. 1140) Provençal
Probably came from Die, north east of Montelimar and was descended from the seigneurial families of the Viennois and Burgundy. 'A chantar m'er de so qu'ieu non volria' is the only song of some 20 known women troubadors to survive with music. Its more personal and realistic tone is characteristic of the women's compositions.

Jane Cooper (1924–) American
The Weather of Six Mornings, her first collection, received the Lamont Award (Academy of American Poets) (1968). Author of *Maps and Windows* (1974), *Threads: Rosa Luxemburg from Prison* (1979). Co-recipient of the Shelley Award of Poetry Society of America, 1978. Retired from teaching and lives in New York.

Jayne Cortez (1936–) American
Born in Arizona. Published several volumes of poetry including *Pissstained Stairs and the Monkey Man's Wares* (1969) and *Coagulations: New and Selected Poems* (1984).

Ida Cox (1889–1968) American
Blues singer and composer. Songs include 'Fogyism', 'Western Union Blues' and 'Tree-Top Tall Papa'.

Marie de France (*c*. 1155–89) French
Also known as Marie de Compiègne. Spent part of her life in England. The author of 103 fables and 12 known *lais* (narrative poems of love and adventure), she was writing mainly around 1170–80.

Sor Juana Ines de la Cruz (1652–95) Mexican
One of the leading Latin American writers, she became a nun at an early age
but was famous for her scholarship, her library and her writings, and
maintained a wide circle of friends. Wrote a historic defence of women's
rights to intellectual freedom against her bishop, but in 1693 renounced her
scholarly pursuits, gave away her books and devoted herself to nursing the
sick. Died in a fever epidemic.

Christine de Pisan (1364–1431) French
The first woman of letters to make a living from her writing. Widowed at the
age of 25 after 10 happy years of marriage to a royal notary, she supported
herself and three children writing songs, ballads, rondeaux and love laments.
She never remarried, and was a champion of Joan of Arc. Her life was beset
with worries over money.

Eunice de Souza (1940–) Indian
Lives in Bombay. Volumes include *Fix* (1979), *Women in Dutch Painting*
(1988), and *Ways of Belonging: Selected Poems* (1990, Polygon). Her poetry has
been much anthologised. She teaches English at the University of Bombay.

Alexis de Veaux (1948–) American
Poet, playwright, novelist, journalist, performance artist. Has written a
biography of Billie Holiday, *Don't Explain* (1980), and *Blue Heat: A Portfolio of
Poems and Drawings* (1985).

Diana Der Hovanessian, American
Of Armenian ancestry, the foremost translator of Armenian poetry. Co-
edited and translated *An Anthology of Armenian Poetry*, with Marzbed Mar-
gossian. Works as visiting poet in Massachusetts schools, has won awards
from PEN and the Poetry Society of America. Her poetry has been translated
and published in the USSR and Europe, as well as published in the USA.

Nuala Ni Dhomnaill (1952–) Irish
Raised in the Gaeltacht, has worked for radio in Eire and Northern Ireland.
Two plays for children; a full-length play was commissioned by the Abbey
Theatre. A prolific writer in Gaelic, her *Fear Suaithinseach* (1984) won the Arts
Council prize for Irish poetry. A dual language version of her *Selected Poems*
appeared from Raven Arts in 1988.

Emily Dickinson (1830–80) American
One of the greatest poets in English, she spent her life in Amherst in her
father's house writing secretly. Of over 1700 poems, only seven were
published in her lifetime. She corresponded with Thomas Wentworth Higginson, who twice visited her. Her chief support was her sister-in-law, Sue
Dickinson, to whom she sent many poems. Higginson, essayist, critic and
editor tried to influence her to write more orthodoxly.

Kiki Dimoula (1931–) Greek
Lives in Athens and works for a bank. Her first book was published in 1952, and she has published four other volumes of poetry.

Blaga Dimitrova (1922–) Bulgarian
Author of nine books of poetry, four novels and three plays. Studied Slavic literature, and has been translated and published in the USA.

Silvia Dobson, British
Lives in California. Alive and working today, Ms Dobson was a friend of Sylvia Beach, Sylvia Townsend Warner, H.D. and others. Her poetry was first published in 1937. She has written many articles on H.D.

H.D. [Hilda Doolittle] (1886–1961) American
Major American poet, born in Pennsylvania, studied at Bryn Mawr. Was engaged to Pound and friend of Carlos Williams. Married Richard Armstrong and lived in Europe. After the break-up of her marriage, she had a relationship with British writer Bryher for the rest of her life. First woman to receive American Academy of Arts and Letters medal; author of many novels and major poetry works, eg *Trilogy*, *Helen in Egypt*.

Rita Dove (1952–) American
Poet and educator, she won the Pulitzer prize for *Thomas and Beulah* (1986). Other volumes of poetry include *Museum* (1983), *The Yellow House on the Corner* (1980) and *The Other Side of the House* (1980).

Alice Dunbar-Nelson (1875–1935) American
Poet, journalist, short-story writer. Poetry uncollected but widely anthologised. Prose includes *Violets and Other Tales* (1895) and *The Goodness of St Roque and Other Stories* (1899).

Helen Dunmore (1952–) English
Born in Yorkshire. She is a nursery teacher, and has two children. Her collections are, *The Apple Fall* (1983), *The Sea Skater* (1986), *The Raw Garden* (1988), all from Bloodaxe Books.

Rachel Blau DuPlessis, American
Author of *Writing Beyond the Ending* (1985); *H.D.: The Career of That Struggle* (1986), *The Pink Guitar: Writing as Feminist Practice* (1990), all works of feminist criticism. Poems – *Wells* (1980), *Tabula Rosa* (1987). Edited the *Selected Letters of George Oppen* (1990) and co-edited *Signets: Reading H.D.* (1990).

Queen Elizabeth I (1533–1603) English
Many poems have been attributed to her, but only two are definitely of her authorship. She read and wrote in several languages, including Greek and Latin. She translated, amongst others, Margaret of Navarre, and Boethius' *Consolation of Philosophy*.

Enheduanna (born *c*. 2300 BC) Sumerian
The first known writer in history whose work has been preserved. 'The exaltation of Inanna' is a sequence of 18 stanzas on cuneiform tablets. She was a priestess of the moon goddess Inanna, and daughter of King Sargon of Agade.

'Ephelia' (born *c*. 1679), English
Poet and playwright, author of *Female Poems on Several Occasions Written by Ephelia* (1679), an unpublished play *The Royal Pair of Coxcombs* (*c*. 1678). The first English 'proto-feminist' poet who also makes mockery of traditional sexual conventions.

Elaine Equi, American
Lives in New York. Author of six collections of poetry, including most recently, *Surface Tension*, published by Coffee House Press.

U.A. Fanthorpe (1929–) English
Educated at Oxford, has held many writer-in-residenceships. *Collected Poems* published in 1986.

Forugh Farrokhzad (1934–67) Iranian
Poet, film-maker and critic. Married at the age of 17, had one son. Lived in a leper colony for a time. A major figure in modern Persian poetry, especially for her willingness to speak frankly about love, sex, society and the self. Author of five collections of poetry.

Elaine Feinstein (1930–) British
Born in Lancashire of Russian-Jewish parents; translator and biographer of Marina Tsvetaeva; novelist and poet, most recent collection *Badlands*, 1986. Author of eight novels, two biographies and five collections of poetry. Lives in London; fellow of the Royal Society of Literature since 1980.

Alison Fell (1944–) Scottish
Born in Dumfries. Novelist and children's writer; involved with Women's Theatre; lives in London. Author of *Kisses for Mayakovsky* which won the Alice Hunt Bartlett Prize for Poetry in 1984, *The Grey Dancer* (1981) (children's novel), *Every Move You Make* (1984) and *The Bad Box* (1987) (novels) *The Crystal Owl* (poems).

Anne Finch, Countess of Winchilsea (1661–1720) English
Widely recognised as a poet with a large circle of literary friends, her work was supported by her husband, an opponent of the House of Orange; they lived between town and country in difficult circumstances. She opposed the prevailing denigration of women writers.

Veronica Forrest-Thomson (1947–1975) Scottish
Poet and critical theorist; author of *Poetic Artifice: A Theory of Twentieth-Century Poetry* (1978). In her lifetime she published four collections of poetry;

posthumously *On the Periphery* appeared from Street Editions (1976). *Collected Poems and Translations* have now appeared from Allardyce Barnett (1990).

Eleni Fourtouni, Greek
Born in Sparta, has lived in USA since 1953. Studied in Maine and is a translator, poet and editor. Has one son and one daughter.

Cynthia Fuller (1948–) English
Lives in Durham with her two children, teaches adult education, women's studies and creative writing courses. Poet and editor of *Writing Women*, she has written one novel and her work has appeared in many magazines.

Gloria Fuertes (1920–) Spanish
Born and lived most of her life in Madrid. Many publications, of poetry, fiction, stories and plays for children. Organised readings by women and has given many herself. Edited a review, worked as a secretary. Her mother was a seamstress, her father a factory worker. She has said she was not born into privilege, but into poetry. Works include *Que Estás en la Tierra* (1962), *Antologica Poetica* (1970), *Obras Incompletas* (1981).

Sylva Gaboudikan (1919–) Armenian
Besides being the leading woman poet in Yerevan, Armenia, she is an articulate activist for Armenian land held by Azeri Turks.

Katherine Gallagher (1935–) Australia
Born in Victoria, Australia. Writing poetry since 1965; now lives in London. Books include *The Eye's Circle*, (1975), *Tributaries of the Love Song*, (1978), *Passengers to the City* (1985) and *Fish Rings on Water* (1989).

Tess Gallagher (1943–) American
Was married to the short story writer and poet Raymond Carver. Since his death has been working on a book of poems and a novel. She holds the Mackey Chair for fiction at Beloit College, Wisconsin. Books include *The Lover of Horses* (short stories), *Instruction to the Double* (1976), *Under Stars* (1978), *Willingly* (1984) and *Amplitude, New and Selected-Poems*.

Sarah Gorham, American
Her first collection of poems *Don't Go Back To Sleep* (1989) was published by Galileo Press in 1989. Her work has also appeared in *Antaeus, The Nation, Poetry Northwest* and other magazines. She is the recipient of grants from the states of Delaware and Connecticut, and the Kentucky Foundation for Women. In 1983, she won the Poetry Society of America's Gertrude Claytor Prize.

Shushanig Gourghenian (1876–1927) Armenian
Part of Eastern Armenia's literary resurgence, she wrote mainly poems of social protest, against living and working conditions, the position of women and oppression by the Turks, as well as many love lyrics.

Judy Grahn, American
Grew up in Chicago and southern New Mexico. Co-founded in 1970 the first all-women's press. Teaches courses in women's writing, poetry, literature and gay and lesbian studies. Widely translated and anthologised. *Another Mother Tongue: Gay Words, Gay Worlds* was chosen as Gay Book of the Year by the American Library Association in 1985.

Janet Gray (1948–) American
Lived in Korea and India, 1956–60, where her parents were Quaker peace workers. Worked in the peace movement in the 1970s. Now working for her doctorate in English literature at Princeton. *Flaming Tail Out of the Ground Near Your Farm* and other books published by Illuminati, Los Angeles.

Adrienne Greer (1965–) American.
Member of Summer Arts Institute. Graduated from Sara Lawrence College. Doing post-graduate work in creative writing.

Carole C. Gregory (1945–) American
Now teaches writing at the Borough of Manhattan Community College and at New York University. She has recently finished a poetry book entitled *For a Lifetime*.

Ann Griffiths (1776–1805) Welsh
Lived and wrote in Dlwar Fach, mid-Wales. Finest Welsh poet of the 19th century, her hymns derive from her wholehearted Methodist belief and were part of the community in which she lived. They were dictated to Ruth, her maid, whose husband transcribed them. She is known as author of about 24 surviving hymns and fragments.

Angelina Weld Grimké (1880–1958) American
Poet and playwright. Poems widely anthologised, eg. in *Caroling Dusk: An Anthology of Verse by Negro Poets*, ed. Countee Cullen (1927).

Emily Grosholz, American
She is associate Professor of Philosophy at Pennsylvania State University. She has published two books of poetry, *The River Painter* (Univ. of Illinois, 1984) and *Shores and Highlands* (Princeton Univ. 1988). She has recently received an Ingram Merrill Award and a Guggenheim Fellowship for poetry.

Marilyn Hacker (1942–) American
The author of six books of poetry, most recently *Going Back to the River* (1990) and *Love, Death and the Changing of the Seasons* (1986). Onlywomen will publish her selected poems 1980–89 *The Hang Glider's Daughter* in 1990. Edited feminist literary magazine *13th Moon* from 1982–6. She lives in New York and Paris.

Joy Harjo (1951–) American
Member of the Creek tribe, she lives in Tulsa, Oklahoma. Has published three books of poems, most recently, *She Had Some Horses*.

Frances E.W. Harper (1825–1911) American
First African-American woman to publish a short story, in 1859. Author of many books of poetry including *Poems on Miscellaneous Subjects* (1854), and a novel *Iola Leroy or Shadows Uplifted* (1892).

Iyamide Hazely, British
Winner of the Minority Arts Group award for poetry in 1984, joint winner of the GLC Black Experience filmscript competition, 1986.

Madge Herron (born *c.* 1917), Irish
Well-known dramatist, her plays have been widely performed. Studied acting in Dublin and at RADA. She was born to a Gaelic-speaking family and studied English at evening classes. Author of *Rory O'Donnell* and many one-act plays for radio; she has said that her poems are millions of years old and do not belong to her.

Selima Hill (1945–), English
Winner of a Cholmondeley award and the 1987 Arvon Poetry/Observer competition. Lives in Dorset with her family. Author of *Saying Hello at the Station* (1984), *My Darling Camel* (1987) and *The Culmination of All Her Secret Longings* (1989).

Frances Horovitz (1938–83) English
Born in London, educated at Bristol University and RADA. *Water Over Stone* (1980), *Snow Light, Water Light* (1983). *Collected Poems* published posthumously, 1985.

Fanny Howe, American
Teaches at University of California (San Diego) and has three children. Published several volumes of poetry and fiction, including *Robson Street, The Vineyard, The Deep North* and *Famous Questions*.

Hroswitha (935–1005) German
'As a writer of Latin drama she stands alone between the classic times and the Miracle plays. She was born into a gentle family and went early to the Ganderseim nunnery where she was educated largely by the Abbess Gerberg. She wrote an unique history for the nuns' use in metrical form.'

Huang O, (1498–1569) Chinese
Daughter of Ming court official, married to a poet and dramatist; her erotic poetry contravened the conventions for women poets.

Erica Hunt, American
Lives in New York. Published work in *Poetics Journal, Idiolects and boundary* amongst other places.

Huong, Ho Xuan, (late 18th Century) Vietnamese
A national poet whose work is studied in the school syllabus. Noted for her defence of women's rights and controversial attacks on polygamy.

Hwang, Chin-I, (1506–1544) Korean
Much admired for her reflective love poetry.

Kathleen Jamie, (1962–) Scottish
Grew up in Midlothian, now lives in Sheffield, won Scottish Arts Council award for her colletion *Black Spiders* (1982) and a Gregory award at the age of 19; studied philosophy at Edinburgh, author of *The Way We Live* (Bloodaxe Books 1987).

Georgia Douglas Johnson (1886–1966) American
Several volumes of poems were published in her lifetime, including *The Heart of a Woman and Other Poems* (1918) and *Bronze, a Book of Verse* (1922).

Helene Johnson (1907–) American
Poems widely anthologised, including in *Caroling Dusk*, and *Opportunity* magazine.

Anna Kamieńska (1920–86) Polish
Trained as a teacher and read Classics. Through the late 40s and 50s she worked as a literary editor. For 25 years she worked as free-lance writer and translator for many languages. Author of more than 15 books of poetry, three novels, literary essays, poems and stories for children. Works published throughout Europe, including the USSR. Major editions *Selected Poems* (1971) and *Poems* (1982), both from Warsaw.

Judith Kazantzis (1940–) English
Poet, artist and short-story writer, member of the Women's Literature Collective. Books include *Minefield* (1977), *Wicked Queen* (1980), *Touch Papers* (with Michelene Wandor and Michèle Roberts, 1982), *Let's Pretend* (1984), *Poem for Guatemala* (1985), and *Flame Tree* (1988).

Helen Kidd (1946–) British
Lives in Oxford; is researching into contemporary women poets, teaches at Oxford Polytechnic and looks after her three children. She is organiser of the Old Fire Station Poetry Workshop and co-editor of New Poetry from Oxford.

Sarah Kirsch (1939–) German
Born in GDR, left to live in West Germany in 1977 after opposing the government over the poet Wolf Biermann's expulsion. Lives in northern Germany with her son where the landscape plays an important part in her poetic world. Acknowledged the leading woman poet writing in German, she has won many prizes. Volumes of translations of her work into English will be appearing soon in Britain. *Schneewärme* (1989) is her most recent volume.

Carolyn Kizer (1925–) American
Born in Washington, she now lives in California, poet, educator and critic, she considers herself to be a 'political poet'. Author of seven collections of

poetry including *Mermaids and The Basement: Poems for Women* (1984) and *Yin: New Poems* (1984), winner of the 1985 Pulitzer Prize for poetry.

Khosrovidought Koghtnatsi (8th century) Armenian
She was the daughter of a ruling prince in Koghten. This poem was written for her martyred brother, Vahan who died defending Christianity.

Ono no Komachi (832–880) Japanese
Legendary figure, one of the earliest Heian courtwomen/poets. (Heian-kyow was the old name for Kyoto, the capital of ancient Japan – 1000 years ago a more civilised and populous city than any in Europe.) The poems were part of a ritual of romance which was a central feature of Japanese court life in the golden age. Ono no Komachi was both the outstanding poet and a very beautiful woman. She died in abject poverty, forgotten, outside the citywalls.

Maxine Kumin (1925–) American
Poet, essayist, novelist and author of 20 books for children. First collection (1961) was winner of the Pulitzer prize for poetry, 1973. Books include *The Long Approach* (poems, 1985) *To Make a Prairie* (essays, 1979) and *Why Can't We Live Together Like Civilised Human Beings* (stories, 1982).

Joanne Kyger (1934–) American
Poet and performance artist. Lived for some time in Japan. Sees herself as a West-coast poet, but with affinities to the younger New York poets. Author of many publications, *The Tapestry and the Web* (1965), *Joanne* (1970), *Desecho Notebook* (1971), *All This Every Day* (1975). Her *Japan and India Journal: 1960–64* was published in 1981, and *Going On* (selected poems, 1958–80) in 1983.

Louise Labé (1525–66) French
From Lyons, the daughter and wife of ropemakers, she was a fine horse-woman and the centre of the Lyons school of poetry. A proto-feminist, she was influenced by Petrarch and some of her poems foreshadow Metaphysical works. Amongst her works are 24 sonnets, three elegies and a Debate between 'Folie' et 'Amour'.

Grace Lake, English
Lives in Cambridge where she is studying English. Mother of three children, has given a number of readings. Poems have appeared in many magazines, including *Slate, The News, Poetical Histories, Archeus, Constant Red: Mingled Damask and Archeus*.

V.R. Lang (1924–56) American
One of the leading young writers of the Poets Theatre in Cambridge, Massachusetts in the early 50s. Poet, editor, director, producer, actress, friend of Frank O'Hara and Alison Lurie. Married to Bradley Phillips.

Lady Anne Lindsay (1750–1825) Scottish
Anne Barnard, daughter of the Earl of Balcarres.

Jelena Lengold (1959–) Yugoslavian
Lives and works as a translator, broadcaster and critic in Belgrade. Has published four books of poetry, *The Collapse of Botany* (1982), *Spindle* (1984), *Poppy Territory* (1986) and *The Passing of an Angel* (1989).

Denise Levertov (1923–) American
Born in England of a Welsh mother and a Russian-Jewish father, she emigrated to USA with her American husband in 1948. Her first book was *The Double Image* (1946); of her many publications since then the most notable are *Collected Earlier Poems 1940–60*, (1979), *Poems 1960–67* (1983) and *Selected Poems* (1986). She has taught at Universities in New York, California and Massachusetts.

Liz Lochhead (1947–) Scottish
Born in Motherwell, a prolific dramatist, reviewer and writer. Studied painting at Glasgow School of Art. Her plays include a Scots' translation of Molière's *Tartuffe*, and work for TV, radio and stage. Works include *Memo for Spring, The Grimm Sisters, Now and Then, True Confessions and New Clichés* (theatre pieces), *Dreaming Frankenstein* and *Collected Poems* (1984).

Audre Lorde (1934–) American
Poet and essayist, she has many volumes published, including *Coal* (1976), *The Black Unicorn* (1978), *Chosen Poems, Old and New* (1983). Prose works include *The Cancer Journals* and *Sister Outsider: Essays and Speeches* (1984).

Amy Lowell (1874–1925) American
Poet, essayist, translator, editor and biographer, her first volume of poetry was published in 1912. From 1915–17 she edited 3 important anthologies of Imagist poetry.

Mina Loy (1882–1966) English
Poet and artist associated with the literary and visual avant-garde in Paris, Florence and New York between 1910 and 1930. One of the leading experimental women poets, she married Stephen Hawers, then Dadaist artist and prize-fighter Arthur Cravan and supported herself and her children by, amongst other things, designing hats and lampshades. Early admirers of her work were T.S Eliot, Yvor Winters and Ezra Pound. She lived most of her life in obscurity in New York. In 1982 Roger L. Conover and the Jargon Society republished her Collected Works, *The Last Lunar Baedeker*.

Liliane Lijn
A sculptor by profession, she has lived in London since 1966 and her large, frequently kinetic works can be seen in many public places in Britain. She has given many readings and performances of her writings in London and elsewhere. Thames & Hudson published her *Crossing Map* in 1983.

Susan Ludvigson, American
Lives half the year in France, half in USA where she teaches. Her books

include *Northern Lights, The Swimmer, The Beautiful Noon of No Shadow*, and most recently, *To Find the Gold* (all from Louisiana State University Press).

Naomi Long Madgett (1923–) American
Lives in Detroit, Michigan. She is the author of several books of poetry including *Pink Ladies in the Afternoon* (1978) and *Octavia and Other Poems* (1988).

Margaret, Duchess of Newcastle (1624–74) English
Poet, playwright, biographer, she wrote many books of orations, letters, utopian fantasy, her own autobiography and a life of her husband, Works include *Poems and Fancies* (1963), *Plays* (1662), *CCXI Sociable Letters* (1664).

Daphne Marlatt Canadian
She wrote thirteen books of poetry and prose, including *Steveston* (1984), *How to Hug a Stone* (1983), *Touch to My Tongue* (1984), *Double Negative* (with Betsy Warland, 1988), and *Ana Historic* (1988). She is editor of *Tessera*, a feminist journal, and Professor of Women's Studies at Simon Fraser University.

Bernadette Mayer, American
Poet and editor, author of 14 collections, her *Sonnets* have been praised by poets such as John Ashberry, Jackson Maclow and Anne Waldman, amongst others. Her books include *The Golden Book of Words* (1978), *Midwinter Day* (1982), *Utopia* (1983), *Mutual Aid* (1985). *The Formal Field of Kissing* is forthcoming.

Christian McEwen (1956–) British
She was born in London, grew up in Scotland, and now lives in New York, on the Lower East Side. She studied at Cambridge and Berkeley, and has held many jobs including gardener, teacher of creative writing, literacy adviser and construction worker. She has edited *Naming the Waves: Contemporary Lesbian Poetry* (Virago, 1988) and has poems widely published in magazines, including *Granta* and *Sinister Wisdom*.

Medbh McGuckian (1950–) Irish
She was born and lives in Belfast. Winner of the National Poetry Competition 1979, and the Gregory Award 1980, she is writer-in-residence at Queen's College, Belfast. Her books include, *The Flower Master* (1982), *Venus and The Rain* (1984), *On Ballycastle Beach* (1988), all from Oxford University Press.

Medaksé (1933–) Armenian
Lives in Yerevan. Considered the 'working woman's poet', she is a feminist and author of over a dozen volumes. She is a popular poetry performer.

Memphis Minnie (born *c.* 1900) American
A blues singer and composer, she played her own accompaniment on the guitar 'like a man'. She wrote amongst other songs, *'Frisco Town, Memphis Minnie Jitis Blues, Killer Diller* and *Nothing in Rambling*.

Charlotte Mew (1869–1928) English
She lived mainly in London; her poems were published by Harold Monro's
Poetry Bookshop and in *The Yellow Book*, and she was described by Thomas
Hardy as the best living woman poet of the time. She was awarded a civil list
pension; was deeply devoted to her friend Mary Sinclair; suffered ill health,
poverty and depression which led her to commit suicide after her sister's
death. Her *Collected Poems and Prose* are published by Carcanet (1982) and
edited by Val Warner.

Edna St Vincent Millay (1892–1950) American
She graduated from Vassar 1917, moved to New York, worked as an actress
and playwright with the Provincetown Players while writing and translating.
Her first collection *Renascence* (1917) was awarded the Pulitzer Prize 1922.
One of America's first poets to win a mass audience for serious writing, her
popularity was at its height in the 1920s.

Alice Milligan (1866–1953) Irish
Member of the Gaelic League, she founded *The Northern Patriot* and *Shan Van
Vocht*. Wrote plays for the Abbey Theatre, including *The Last Feast of Fianna*,
and a biography of Wolf Tone.

Lilian Mohin, American/English
Works at Onlywomen Press of which she is a co-founder. She has written:
'My work is addressed to women, is intended as lesbian poetry'. Co-editor of,
amongst other works, *One Foot on the Mountain: British Feminist Poetry
1969–79*, and *Beautiful Barbarians: Lesbian Feminist Poetry* and *Gossip*, a journal
of lesbian feminist ethics.

Marianne Moore (1887–1972) American
Lived in New York, received many honours for her poetry, including in one
year the Pulitzer Prize, the Bollinger Prize and the National Book Award.
Educated at Bryn Mawr, she established her reputation as a poet by 1925.
Edited the influential literary magazine *The Dial* (1926–9). Her work was
highly praised by T.S. Eliot and Ezra Pound amongst others. An avid baseball
fan she attended many games; the Ford Motor Co. asked her to name a car –
and rejected her suggestion.

Geraldine Monk (1952–) English
Born in Blackburn, Lancs, she now lives in Sheffield. Her collections include:
Long Wake (1979), *Spreading the Cards* (1980), *Animal Crackers* (1984), *Qua-
quaversals* (1990). *Selected Poems* forthcoming (1992).

Janet Montefiore, English
Teaches at the University of Kent and is the author of *Feminism and Poetry*:
Language, Experience, Identity in Women's Writing, (1987) and *In a Glass and
Other Poems*.

Robin Morgan (1941–) Canadian
Writer and international lecturer on feminism. Works include *Monster Poems* (1972), *Lady of the Beasts* (1976), *Going Too Far: The Personal Chronicle of a Feminist*. She describes herself as 'an artist and a political being'. She lives in New York.

Caroline Oliphant, Lady Nairne (1776–1845) Scottish
Daughter of the Laird of Gask, she used the pseudonym Mrs Bogan of Bogan, and wrote many Jacobite songs.

Leslea Newman (1955–) American
In addition to her own collection of poetry *Love Me Like You Mean It* (1987), she has edited a book of poetry called *Bubbe Meisehs by Shayneh Maidelehs: An Anthology of Poetry by Jewish Granddaughters about our Grandmothers*. Her latest collection of fiction is called *Secrets*.

Grace Nichols, Britain/Guyana
Short story writer, journalist, novelist and poet, winner of the Commonwealth Poetry Prize, and author of two books for children. Her titles include *Fat Black Woman's Poems* (1984) and *Whole of a Morning Sky* (1986). Her most recent work is *Lazy Thoughts of a Lazy Woman* (1989). She lives in Brighton with her husband, the poet John Agard, and her daughter.

Caroline Norton (1808–77) Irish
Caroline Elizabeth Sarah Norton was the granddaughter of Richard Sheridan. She was a novelist, pamphleteer and campaigner. Author of *English Laws for Women in the Nineteenth Century*. She separated from her jealous husband in 1840.

Nossis of Locri (born *c.* 300BC) Greek
Lived in a Greek colony in S. Italy having an unusual matrilineal aristocracy. Her epigrams reflect a female world centred around the worship of Hera and Aphrodite. A follower of the Sapphic poetic tradition, she is known for only 12 poems. H.D., the American poet, wrote her own poem called 'Nossis', adapting the first epigram.

Alice Notley, American
'All I do is write poems.' Alice Notley lives with her two sons and is the author of many books of poetry. She has given readings throughout the USA and Europe. Works include *At Night the States* (1988) and *Two Poems*.

Joyce Carol Oates, American
Novelist, short-story writer and poet, she is author of over 30 books of poetry, fiction and essays. On the faculty of Princeton University. Most recent novel *American Appetites* (1989); *Invisible Woman: New and Selected Poems* appeared in 1982.

Rosie Orr, English
Poet, artist and playwright, teaches English and lives in Oxford with her two children.

Alicia Ostriker, American
Poet, critic and author of seven volumes of poetry, *Stealing the Language: The Emergence of Women's Poetry in America*. Her recent volume of poems, *The Imaginary Lover*, won the William Carlos Williams prize in 1986. Her latest book is *Green Age*. She is Professor of English at Rutgers University.

Ruth Padel, British
Author of two books of poetry *Alibi* (1985) and *Summer Snow* (1990), her work has appeared in many magazines such as the *Kenyon Review* and *The Times Literary Supplement*. She is currently working on a book on Ancient Greek ideas of what is inside people, 'Feelings, demons and biology'. She has one daughter.

Dorothy Parker (1893–1967) American
Poet, reviewer, story-writer and wit. Her earliest poetry was sold to *Vogue*, for which she then worked. Drama critic of *Vanity Fair* magazine, reviewer for *The New Yorker* and *Esquire*. Collections include *Not So Deep as a Well*, and *Enough Rope* (both poetry) and *Here Lies* (stories). Twice married, she worked in Hollywood with Alan Campbell, her second husband. After his death she took to drink and died alone in a hotel room in Manhattan.

Molly Peacock, American
Author of three books of poetry, *Take Heart* (1989), *Raw Heaven* (1984), and *Live Apart* (1980), she was visiting professor at a number of universities, President of the Poetry Society of America. She is a learning specialist.

Katherine Philips (1631–64) English
Daughter of a merchant, established a literary salon and lived the life of a successful literary lady. Known as 'Orinda', was well-known as a translator (e.g. Corneille's *Pompey*); one volume of poetry published during her lifetime.

Alejandra Pizarnik (1936–72) Argentinian
Author of seven collections of poetry, acclaimed as one of the leading Latin American poets, she studied painting in Paris, and shocked her society by her bisexuality. Susan Bassnet is preparing a translation of her poems.

Sylvia Plath (1932–63) American
The major Ms resources for her are at the Lilly Library, Indiana and the Smith College Neilson Library. Her *Collected Poems* (1981), *Journals* (1982), and recently the biography by Anne Stevenson, *Bitter Fame* (1989), are all available, as is her correspondence 1950–63, novel, *The Bell Jar*, and two prose collections. Born in Massachusetts and educated at Smith College, she lived in England after her marriage and had two children.

Marsha Prescod, Britain/Guyana
She came to Britain in the 1950s and is author of *Land of Rope and Tory*.

Rabi'a the Mystic (712–801) Persian
Her full name was Rabi'a al Adawiyya, a celebate mystic and Islamic saint who lived in the desert as a hermit and ascetic, writing ecstatic religious poetry and prose. She was accredited with many miracles.

Gertrude 'Ma' Rainey (1886–1939) American
Blues singer and composer, born Pridgett, she married Will 'Pa' Rainey of a travelling minstrel show and they travelled the tent-show circuit with their song-and-dance act 'Rainey & Rainey, the assassinators of the Blues'. After they separated she made her name in the 1920s on Paramount recordings.

Deborah Randell (1957–) English
Lives in Kirkwall, in the Orkneys, Winner of 1987 Bloodaxe Poetry competition, with the *Sin-Eater*.

Jessie Redmon Fauset (1882–1961) American
Poet, novelist and editor. Poems widely anthologised, e.g. *Poetry of the Negro* (1949), ed. L. Hughes and A. Bontemps. Novels include *Plum Bun* (1929) and *The Chinaberry Tree* (1931).

Carlyle Reedy (1938–) American/British
Born in Virginia, USA; long time resident in London, where she works in 'Eventstructural live poetry/visual art Theatre'. Performs all over Europe and in USA. Her published works in limited editions include *Sculpted in this World* and *The Orange Notebook*.

Adrienne Rich (1929–) American
Graduated from Radcliffe and has lived in New York City since 1966. Influential lesbian feminist writer and lecturer, her many works include *On Lies Secrets and Silence* (prose), *Of Woman Born: Motherhood as Experience and Institution*; and *The Fact of a Doorframe: Poems Selected and New 1950–84*. Mother of three sons, she has been active in civil rights and anti-war movements and in the women's movement as a lesbian.

Denise Riley (1948–) English
Lives in North London, mother of three children, her early poems were published by Street Editions in the 1970s. Historian and philosopher, she has worked at a number of universities including Brown, Princeton and Brisbane. Author of *War in the Nursery: Theories of the Child and Mother*, and *Am I That Name: Feminism and the Category of 'Women' in History*. Virago published *Dry Air*, her selected poems, in 1985.

Michèle Roberts (1947–) English
Novelist and poet, lives and works in London. Author of four novels, including *The Wild Girl* (1984) and *The Book of Mrs Noah* (1987), she has also

written short stories and essays. Poetry includes *Touch Papers* (with Judith Kazantzis and Micheline Wandor   and *The Mirror of the Mother* (1986). Her latest novel is *The Red Kitchen* (1990).

Christina Rossetti (1830–94) English
A devout poet whose *Goblin Market* was one of the key Pre-Raphaelite poems. A painter as well as poet, she was educated by her mother, and lived at home. She had a wide circle of friends. Together with Elizabeth Barrett Browning and Emily Brontë, she is one of England's most important nineteenth-century women poets.

Muriel Rukeyser (1913–80) American
Educated at Vassar, biographer and an important poet of commitment – to women, for civil rights, against fascism and war. Her *Collected Poems* appeared in 1979. She received many awards for her work.

Kate Ruse–Glason, English
Lives in Singapore. Author of *Mountain Poems* (1979).

Sappho (6th century BC) Greek
Little is known about her except that she lived on Lesbos, was a highly regarded poet around whom young women of high birth gathered to study and perhaps take part in the worship of Aphrodite.

Sonia Sanchez (1934–) American
Her books include *Homecoming* (1969); *We a Bad People* (1970) and *Homegirls and Handgrenades* (1984).

May Sarton (1912–) American
Born in Belgium, the author of over 50 books incuding novels, poetry, memoirs and diaries, she considers herself primarily a poet. She has had 18 volumes of poetry published. She lives in Maine.

E.J. Scovell (1907–) English
Books include *The River Steamer* (1956), *The Space Between* and *Listening to Collared Doves*. She began writing in the 1920s; Carcanet published her *Collected Poems* (1988). She is married to an ecologist and has spent time in the West Indies and in the South and Central American rain forests. She lives in Oxford.

Naomi Segal, English
Lives in Cambridge with her two small children where she teaches French literature at St John's College. Author of several books on feminist criticism, she is at present working on a study of mothers in the novel of adultery.

Ntozake Shange (1948–) American
Poet, playwright, dancer, actress, novelist, director and educator. Books include *Nappy Edges* (1978), *A Daughter's Geography* (1983), and *Ridin' the Moon in Texas* – all poetry; *Betsey Brown* (1985), novel; and the choreopoem,

which she also performed, *For coloured girls who have considered suicide when the rainbow is enuf.*

Melanie Silgardo (1956–) Indian
Born in Bombay, she has published a single volume of poems, *Skies of Design* (1985). She works in book publishing and lives in London.

Elizabeth Smart (1913–86) Canadian
After many travels she moved to London during the war. She worked successively as a sub-editor and copywriter for *Vogue* and *House and Garden*, and in advertising for 20 years to support her four children by the poet George Barker. Her best known book is *By Grand Central Station I Sat Down and Wept*; also author of four books of poetry. Her journals are forthcoming.

Bessie Smith (1898–1937) American
Learned her first blues from 'Ma' Rainey. Spent her youth on the road until in the 1920s her recordings brought her fame. Sang in theatres and nightclubs throughout the USA, but in the Depression she was often out of work and penniless. She was killed in a car crash on a tour when she was trying to make a comeback.

Pattie Smith (1946–) American
Singer, composer, writer, performer, she won numerous awards for her recordings, albums include *Horses* (1975), *Radio Ethiopia* (1976), *Easter* (1978), *Wave* (1979). Contributor to *Rock, Rolling Stone* and other magazines. Books include *Seventh Heaven, Witt, Ha! Ha! Houdini* and *Babel*.

Stevie Smith (1902–1971) English
Born in Hull. Poet and novelist, her reputation was established through a series of successful readings in the 1960s. She published three novels and eight collections of poems in her life-time. She lived with her aunt in the same house all her life in London, and worked as a publisher's secretary. She won the Queen's medal for poetry in 1969.

Edith Södergran (1892–1923) Swedish
Born in St Petersburg she was educated at German-speaking schools in Russia. She moved to Finland, then a province of Russia, after her father's death. *Poems* (1916), *The September Lyre* (1918) aroused furious critical response for her experimentalism. Involved with Finnish-Swedish literary circles, she published three more books and died of tuberculosis and malnutrition. Her work has strongly influenced modernists in Sweden and Finland.

Nina Solomon (1964–) American
Educated at Barnard College and awarded the Academy of American Poets prize. She lives in New York, doing graduate work in English literature at Columbia. Her poems have been published in literary magazines.

Anne Spencer (1882–1975) American
Her poetry has been widely anthologised, e.g. in *Caroling Dusk* and *The Crisis* magazine.

Elizabeth Spires (1952–) American
Author of three collections of poetry: *Globe* (1981), *Swan's Island* (1985), *Annonciade* (1989). She lives in Baltimore and teaches at The Johns Hopkins University and Goucher College.

Maura Stanton, American
Author of three books of poetry *Snow on Snow* (1975), *Cries of Swimmers* (1984), and *Tales of the Supernatural* (1988). She teaches at Indiana University.

Gertrude Stein (1874–1946) American
Studied psychology and medicine originally but abandoned it as it bored her. Moved to Paris in 1903 and spent the rest of her life in France with Alice B. Toklas. Friend of Picasso, Braque and other painters, she was a leading experimentalist of the century.

Rita Anyiam St. John, Britain/Nigeria
Currently living with her husband and two children in Nigeria. Has worked for TV, as an editor, part-time lecturer and baker. Author of *Only This Blade of Grass* (unpublished). Shortly returning to live in Manchester.

Anne Stevenson (1933–) American
Born in England, she was educated in USA, but spent most of her adult life in the UK. Author of seven books of poetry, *Bitter Fame, A Life of Sylvia Plath*. Many contributions to the *Times Literary Supplement* and other periodicals. She has held several writing fellowships at Universities. *Selected Poems (1956–86)* was published 1987. She lives in Durham with her husband.

Alfonsina Storni (1892–1938) Argentinian
Born in Switzerland, she was one of the foremost twentieth century South American poets. Her translator writes: 'Her poems reveal her intense desire for equality of the sexes and the rights of women in a time and culture unsympathetic to such aspirations.' She lived in Buenos Aires, and took part in the intellectual and literary life of the capital, the only woman to do so. An educator, she worked for children's theatre.

Sulpicia (*c.* 20BC) Roman
Lived during the reign of Augustus (31BC–AD14), known for only six surviving elegies. Ezra Pound admired her work.

Lady Suo (11th century) Japanese

May Swenson (1919–) American
She has published many volumes of poetry and won awards and fellowships for her work. Her works include *Another Animal, A Cage of Spines, To Mix With Time*, and *Half Sun Half Sleep*.

Janet Sutherland (1957–) English
Lives in London, her work has been widely published in magazines; poetry-editor for *City Limits*. Works for Hackney Council. Author of *Crossing Over* (1983).

Wu Tsao (19th century) Chinese
The daughter and wife of merchants, she is China's best known lesbian poet.

Sara Teasdale (1884–1933) American
She came from a prosperous background and her early poetry attracted attention, but later her work was ignored. She was strongly influenced by Christina Rossetti, whose biography she planned to write. Her last book of poems, *Strange Victory*, appeared in 1933, the same year that she committed suicide.

Sylvia Townsend Warner (1893–1978) English
Musicologist, novelist, short-story writer, translator, biographer and poet, she lived the first part of her life in London, afterwards moving to Dorset where she shared a house with Valentine Ackland. Virago have republished her novels and her *Collected Poems* appeared from Carcanet in 1982 edited by Claire Harman, who also wrote her life. Wendy Mulford wrote a study of her life with Valentine Ackland, their letters and politics. (1988)

Marina Tsvetaeva (1892–1941) Russian
Her life was a struggle against her country. After the revolution she and her husband and children lived first in Prague, then in Paris, in great poverty. She followed her husband back to Russia in 1939 where he was shot on entry. She committed suicide in 1941. Elaine Feinstein has translated her poetry, and written her life, *Captive Lion*.

Nika Turbina (1974–) Russian
A celebrated poet in the USSR – an LP of her poems sold over 30,000 copies. Her first collection *First Draft* won the Golden Lion of Venice prize. Is studying at the same school which Tsvetaeva once attended. *Komsomolskaya Pravda* published her first poems in 1982, when she was eight.

Chase Twichell, American
Has published two collections of poetry, *Northern Spy* (1981), and *The Odds* (1986). *Perdido*, her third, is forthcoming from Farrar Straus & Giroux. She lectures in creative writing at Princeton.

Doina Uricariu (1950–) Romanian
Studied French and Romanian at Bucharest University, works as an editor. She has published five books of poetry and a study of Emil Botta the Romanian poet.

Shadab Vadji, Iranian
She works for the BBC World Service. *Closed Circuit* is her first book to be translated into English.

Patrizia Vicinelli (1943–) Italian
She worked in experimental theatre during early 1960s and was one of the youngest members of 'Gruppo 63'. Also works in cinema and experimental music and has acted in many 'underground' Italian films such as *Virulentis* and

Notte E Il Giorno. Author of '*a. à. A*' (1967). *Apology of a Schizoid Woman* (1979) and *I Fondamenti Dell' Esere* amongst many others.

Gill Vickers (1947–) English
Spent her early years in Somerset and Bristol. The author of one collection *Untitled*: R. Books, Cambridge and Cheltenham, 1969.

Solveig Von Schoultz (1907–) Finnish
Born in Porvoo, she is the leading woman writer in Finland-Swedish, and has written thirteen collections of poetry, from which Anne Born has translated a selection in *Snow & Summers*. Her other works are plays, short stories, autobiographies, a study of child development and a study of her own relationship with her mother; in all more than 30 works. She was awarded the Pro-Finlandia medal in 1980.

Alice Walker (1944–) American
Poet, essayist and novelist. Novels include the Pulitzer Prize-winning *The Color Purple* (1983) and *The Temple of My Familiar* (1989). She has published several books of poetry including *Revolutionary Petunias* (1973), *Good Night, Willie Lee, I'll See You in the Morning* (1984), and *Horses Make a Landscape Look More Beautiful* (1986).

Margaret Walker (1915–) American
Poet, novelist and educator. Her works include *Jubilee* (1966, novel); *For My People* (1942) and *Prophets for a New Day* (1970), both poetry, and a study of Richard Wright (1988). Her *Collected Poems* appeared in 1989.

Michelene Wandor (1940–) British
Poet, playwright and critic. Her *Collected Poems* are due out this year. She has done features on, and dramatisations of Antonia White, Jean Rhys, Jane Austen and Dostoevsky for radio, amongst others. Most recent work Eugene Sue's *The Wandering Jew* at the National Theatre; author and editor of many plays, and of two critical works on theatre and sexual politics.

Diane Ward (1956–) American
She lives in Los Angeles with her small son. Widely represented in anthologies and magazines, she is author of six books of poetry and recipient of several awards. Her most recent collection is *Relation* (Roof Books, NY, 1989).

Anna Wickham (1884–1947) English
After some time in Australia, she spent most of her life in London. Poems published by Harold Monro's Poetry Bookshop and widely anthologised. *The Writings of Anna Wickham: Free Woman and Poet* appeared from Virago, 1984.

Princess Zeb–un–Nissa (1638–1702) Persian
An important patron of scholars and poets, later imprisoned by her father, probably for supporting her brother's rebellion. She was best known for her religious poetry.

Acknowledgements

Every effort has been made to trace copyright holders in all copyright material in this book. The editor regrets if there has been any oversight and suggests the publisher be contacted in any such event. We gratefully acknowledge the following permissions:

Valentine Ackland, 'Teaching to shoot', from *The Nature of the Moment*, Chatto & Windus, 1973. Reprinted by permission of Chatto and Windus/The Hogarth Press, and copyright © The executors, Valentine Ackland Estate, 1973.

Jarl Hammarberg, for permission to reprint extract from 'What Does Your Colour Red Look Like?', by Sonja Åkesson, published in *Modern Swedish Poetry in Translation*, eds Gunnar Harding & Anselm Hollo, University of Minnesota Press, 1979. This translation reprinted by permission and copyright © Anselm Hollo, 1979.

Anna Akhmatova, 'You thought I was that type'; 'I see, I see the crescent moon', reprinted by permission of Bloodaxe Books Ltd from *Anna Akhmatova: Selected Poems*, translated by Richard McKane (Bloodaxe Books, 1989), copyright © this translation Richard McKane 1969, 1989.

Meena Alexander, 'Young Snail', reproduced by permission and copyright © Meena Alexander 1990.

Gillian Allnutt, 'meeting you at an underground station', first published *Spinster*, No. 3, reprinted by permission and copyright © Gillian Allnutt, 1990.

Julia Alvarez, 'Ironing Their Clothes', first published in *The Renewal of the Vision: Voices of Latin American Women Poets 1940–80*, eds. Marjorie Agosin and Cola Franzen, Spectacular Diseases, 1987, reprinted by permission and copyright © Julia Alvarez 1987.

Maya Angelou, 'A Zorro Man', from *Just Give Me a Cool Drink 'Fore I Diiie*, 1971, reprinted by permission of Random House, Inc., and Virago Press, copyright © Maya Angelou 1971.

Tony Conran translator, for [Anon, Welsh], 'The shirt of a lad' [Anon], 'Stanzas for Harp', and 'Expecting The Lord', by Ann Griffiths, all from *Welsh Verse*, edited with an introduction by Tony Conran, Poetry Wales Press, 1986, copyright © this translation Tony Conran 1986.

Dance Song: 'Pretty I am, but I am wretched; Dawn Song: 'On Tuesday my lover and I . . .', Anon, from *Medieval Lyrics of Europe*, edited Willard R. Trask, New American Library and World Publishing Co., Cleveland, copyright © William R. Trask this translation 1969.

Ruth Padel, translator, Cretan Song, 'Invitation', copyright © Ruth Padel; this translation 1990.

Ruth Asher-Pettipher, 'A love like war', copyright © Ruth Asher-Pettipher 1990.

Deletant & Brenda Walker 1988, copyright © 'Accident', this translation Fleur Adcock 1988.

Hélène Cixous, extract from *Vivre L'Orange*, Editions des Femmes, Paris, reprinted by permission the author and publisher, copyright © this translation Anne Liddle and Sarah Cornell 1979.

Gillian Clarke, from 'Letter from a Far Country', from *Letter from a Far Country*, Carcanet Press 1982, reprinted by permission Carcanet Press Ltd, copyright © Gillian Clarke, 1982.

Lucille Clifton, 'Sisters', from *An Ordinary Woman*, Random House, 1974, reprinted by permission, Curtis Brown, New York, copyright © Lucille Clifton, 1974.

Sally Cline, 'Changes', first published in *Naming the Waves: Contemporary Lesbian Poetry*, ed. Christian McEwan, Virago, 1988, reprinted by permission and copyright © Sally Cline, 1988.

Anne Cluysenaar, 'Dark Mothers', from an unpublished work 'Gilgamesh Variations', copyright © Anne Cluysenaar, 1990.

Norma, Cole, 'I think of him as a house and as an ordeal', from *Metamorphopsia* Potes & Poets Press, Connecticut, 1988. Reprinted by permission and copyright © Norma Cole, 1988.

Jane Cooper, 'Conversation by the Body's Light', from *Scaffolding, New & Selected Poems*, Anvil Press Poetry, London. Reprinted by permission publisher and poet, copyright © Jane Cooper 1984.

Jayne Cortez, 'Rose Solitude (for Duke Ellington)' from *Coagulations: New and Selected Poems*, Pluto Press, 1984. Reprinted by permission and copyright © Jayne Cortez 1990.

Nuala ni Dhomnaill, 'Labysheedy (the silken bed)', from *Selected Poems*, tr. Nuala Ni Dhomnaill, Raven Arts, Dublin, 1986. Reprinted by permission of Raven Arts and the author, copyright © Nuala ni Dhomnaill 1986.

Stephen Haynes, translator, for 'I must sing of that which I would rather not' by the Comtesse de Dia. copyright © this translation Stephen Haynes 198

Eilis Dillon, translator, for 'Lament for Art O'Leary', by Eibhlin Dhubh ní Chonaill, copyright © this translation Eilis Dillon 1970, 1990.

Doubleday (Bantam Doubleday Dell Publishing Group Inc.) for permission to reprint from *Women on Love* by Evelyn Sullerot: Marie de France, 'Love is a wound within the body'; Christine de Pisan, 'A sweet thing is marriage'; Louise Labe, 'You are alone my evil and my good', copyright © these translations Helen R. Lane 1979.

Sor Juana Ines de la Cruz, 'Verses from a Satirical Romance', copyright © this translation Judith Thurman 1978.

Eunice de Souza, 'From you I have understood'; 'Alibi', from *Women in Dutch Painting*, published Praxix, Bombay 1988, and *Ways of Belonging: Selected Poems* published Polygon Press, Edinburgh 1990. By permission of the author, copyright © 1988, 1990.

Alexis de Veaux, 'The Sisters', from *Gay & Lesbian Poetry in Our Times*, eds. Carl Morse and Joan Larkin, St Martins Press, NY, copyright © Alexis de Veaux, 1988.

Elaine Feinstein, 'Home', from *Badlands*, reprinted by permission Century Hutchinson Ltd, and the author, copyright © Elaine Feinstein 1986.

Alison Fell, 'Supper', from *Kisses for Mayakovsky*, reprinted by permission Peake Associates and author, copyright © Alison Fell 1984.

Veronica Forrest-Thomson, 'Sonnet, "My love, if I write a song for you"', from *On the Periphery*, first published in Street Editions, Cambridge 1976, and reprinted in *Collected Poems and Translations*, Allardyce/Barnett, 1990, copyright © Jonathan Culler, the estate of Veronica Forrest-Thomson 1976, 1990.

Forugh Farrokhzad, 'Couple', from *Another Birth: Selected Poems of Forugh Farrokhzad*, Albany Press, Middle Eastern Series, Ca., reprinted by permission and copyright © this translation Hasan Javadi and Susan Sallee 1981.

Eleni Fourtouni, 'In a dream'; *Contemporary Greek Women Poets*, ed. Eleni Fourtouni, Thelphini Press, copyright © this translation Eleni Fourtouni 1978.

Gloria Fuertes, 'When I Hear Your Name'; 'I think table and I say chair', from *Off the Map*, reprinted by permission Wesleyan University Press, copyright © this translation Philip Levine and Ada Long 1984.

Cynthia Fuller, 'Fire-Roses', copyright © Cynthia Fuller 1990.

Katherine Gallagher, 'Firstborn', from *Passengers to the City*, Hale & Ironmonger, Sidney, 1985/Forest Books, London. Reprinted by permission Forest Books and copyright © Katherine Gallagher, 1985.

Tess Gallagher, 'All Day the Light Is Clear', from *Amplitude*, Graywolf Press. Reprinted by permission and copyright © Tess Gallagher, 1990.

Sarah Gorham, 'My car slides off the road', from *Don't Go Back to Sleep* 1989, Galileo Press Ltd, reprinted by permission and copyright © Sarah Gorham 1989.

Judy Grahn, from 'Confrontations with the Devil in the Form of Love', from *The Work of A Common Woman: Collected Poetry (1964–77)*, reprinted by permission The Crossing Press, Freedom, Ca., and copyright © Judy Grahn 1984.

Janet Gray, untitled: 'However heavy the walls of love . . .'; 'Not that miracles . . .', first published in *Mirage*, ed. Dodie Bellamy, 1989. Reprinted by permission and copyright © Janet Gray 1989.

Adrienne Greer, 'Constantly', from 'Faith & Pornography', copyright © Adrienne Greer, 1989.

Carole C. Gregory, 'Love Letter', first published in *Conditions 5*, Aug. 1979, reprinted by permission the author and copyright © Carole C. Gregory 1979.

Angelina Weld Grimké, 'El Beso', 'At April', from *Negro Poets and Their Poems*, ed. Robert T. Kerlin, Associated Publishers Inc, Washington DC, 1935, reprinted by permission of the Moorland Spingarn Research Centre, Howard University, Washington, repository of the Grimké papers.

Emily Grosholz, 'On Spadina Avenue', first published in *The Hudson Review* Vol. XLII, No 3 Autumn 89. Reprinted by permission and copyright © Emily Grosholz, 1989.

Forest Books, reprinted by permission publisher and translator, copyright © this translation Susan Bassnett and Piotr Kuhiwczak, 1988.

Judith Kazantzis, 'What idiots lovers are', from *Let's Pretend*, reprinted by permission, and copyright © Judith Kazantzis 1984.

Helen Kidd, 'Meanwhile Cesario dancing', copyright © Helen Kidd, 1985.

Sarah Kirsch, 'Wintermusik', from *Schneewärme*, copyright © Deutsche Verlags-Anstalt, Stuttgart, reprinted by permission, copyright © this translation Wendy Mulford and Anthony Vivis 1989. Sarah Kirsch, 'Incantation', from *Zaubersprüche*, copyright © Langewiesche-Brandt 1975, reprinted by permission copyright © this translation Anthony Vivis 1989.

Carolyn Kizer, 'What the bones know', from *The Nearness of You*, reprinted by permission, Copper Canyon Press, Washington, copyright © Carolyn Kizer 1986.

Ono no Komachi, 'When my desire', reprinted with permission of Charles Scribners Sons, an imprint of Macmillan Publishing Company, from *The Ink Dark Moon*, translated by Jane Hirschfield and Izumi Shikibu, copyright © This translation 1986, 1987, 1988 Jane Hirschfield.

Maxine Kumin, 'After Love', from *The Nightmare Factory*. All rights reserved. Reprinted by permission. Copyright © 1970 by Maxine Kumin.

Joanne Kyger, 'These several selves that move one self around,' from *Trip Out & Fall Back*, Arif Pres, Berkeley. Reprinted by permission and copyright © Joanne Kyger 1974.

Grace Lake, untitled, 'is he painting with tips', copyright © Grace Lake, 1990.

V.R. Lang, 'A Lovely song for Jackson', from *V.R. Lang: Poems & Plays*, with a memoir by Alison Lurie, Heinemann Ltd, London. Reprinted by kind permission & copyright © 1962 Bradley Phillips.

Jelena Lengold, 'Passion', Menard Press, reprinted by permission poet and translator, copyright © this translation Richard Burns 1989.

Denise Levertov, 'Our bodies', from *O Taste and See*, reprinted by permission New Directions Publishing Corporation, copyright © Denise Levertov Goodman, 1963.

Liliane Lijn, 'Out the you of yesterday', from *Six Throws of Oracular Keys*, Unfinitude, Editions de la Nepe, Paris, reprinted by permission of the author, copyright © Liliane Lijn, 1981.

Liz Lochhead, 'Tam Lin's Lady'; 'Sundaysong', from *Dreaming Frankenstein*, Polygon Press, Edinburgh, 1984, reprinted by permission the publisher, copyright © Liz Lochhead 1984.

Audre Lorde, 'Now that I am forever with child'; from *Chosen Poems Old and New*, W.W. Norton, 1982; 'Sisters in arms', from *Our Dead Behind Us*, W.W. Norton, 1986. Reprinted by permission W.W. Norton and Co. Inc, courtesy the author and copyright © Audre Lorde 1982, 1986, 1976, 1974, 1973, 1970, 1968.

Mina Loy, 'Love songs to Joannes' (1–4), reprinted courtesy of the Jargon Society, Highlands, North Carolina, which published The Complete Writings of Mina Loy in

1982, *The Last Lunar Baedeker*, ed. by Roger L. Conover, copyright © 1982 The Jargon Society Inc.

Susan Ludvigson, 'Paris Aubade', from *To Find Gold*, Louisiana State University Press, reprinted by permission, copyright © Susan Ludvigson 1990.

Naomi Long Madgett, 'Black woman', from *Pink Ladies in the Afternoon*, Lotus Press Inc, Detroit 1972, reprinted by permission and copyright © Naomi Long Madgett 1972.

Daphne Marlatt, 'Long time coming', from *What Matters, Writing 1968–70*, Coach House Press, Toronto, 1980. Reprinted by permission and copyright © Daphne Marlatt, 1980.

Bernadette Mayer, 'Sonnet'– 'Everyone makes love to their bereft & go,' *Sonnets*, Tender Buttons, NY, 1989. Reprinted by permission and copyright © Bernadette Mayer, 1989.

Christian McEwen, '2 Wren St'; from *Naming the Waves: Contemporary Lesbian Poetry*, ed. C. McEwen, Virago, 1988, reprinted by permission and copyright © Christian McEwan 1988. 'Love Poem: Growing Down'; 'And Sunday Morning', copyright © Christian McEwan 1990.

Medbh McGuckian, 'The weaver-girl' first published in *The Penguin Book of Contemporary British Poetry*, eds. Blake Morrison and Andrew Motion, Penguin, reprinted by permission and copyright © Medbh McGuckian 1982.

Edna St. Vincent Millay, 'Intention to escape from him'; 'Theme and Variations' (1,2) from *Collected poems*, Harper & Row, copyright © 1939, 1976 by Edna St. Vincent Millay and Norma Millay Ellis. Reprinted by permission of Elizabeth Barnett, Literary Executor.

Alice Milligan, 'The house of the apple trees', from *Poems*, Dublin, 1953, reprinted by permission of the publishers Gill & Macmillan, Dublin, and of A.A. Kelly ed. *Pillars of the House*, op. cit, copyright © 1987.

Lilian Mohin, 'traces, fine bird prints', from *Cracks*, Onlywomen Press, reprinted by permission and copyright © Lilian Mohin, 1986.

Geraldine Monk, 'Stump cross – The long wait', from *Long Wake* (Writers Forum/Pirate Press) reprinted by permission and copyright © Geraldine Monk, 1982.

Janet Montefiore, 'The mistress to her lover', copyright © Janet Montefiore 1990.

Marianne Moore, 'The lion in love', translated from *The Fables of La Fontaine*, *The Complete Poems*, The Macmillan Co./The Viking Press, copyright © the executors of the Estate of Marianne Moore 1954, 1967.

Robin Morgan, 'Survival', first published in *Moving to Antarctica*, ed. Margaret Kaminski, Dustbooks, California, 1975, reprinted by permission and copyright © Robin Morgan, 1975.

Leslea Newman, 'Possibly', from *Love Me Like You Mean It*, Herbooks, California, reprinted by permission of and copyright © Leslea Newman 1987.

Grace Nichols, 'Love act'; 'I go to meet him', from I *Is a Long Memoried Woman*,

Caribbean Cultural International, 1983, reprinted by permission Karnak House London, publisher Amon Saba Saakana, copyright © Grace Nichols 1983.

Alice Notley 'Mornings', 'Untitled' ('Beginning with a stain, as the Universe did perhaps'), copyright © Alice Notley 1990.

Joyce Carol Oates, 'How gentle', reprinted by permission Joyce Carol Oates, copyright © 1982 Ontario Review Press.

Rosie Orr, 'Moon song', copyright © Rosie Orr 1989.

Alicia Ostriker, 'Extraterrestrial: A Wedding Poem for Nina and "John"', Jan 2 1989; copyright © Alicia Ostriker, 1989.

Ruth Padel, 'Watercourse', from *Summer Snow*, Century Hutchinson, 1990, reprinted by permission and copyright © Ruth Padel 1990.

Dorothy Parker, 'Comment': 'One perfect rose'; 'Chant for Dark Hours'; 'Theory'; from *The Portable Dorothy Parker*, Penguin 1976, reprinted by permission Gerald Duckworth & Co. Ltd. and Viking Press, copyright © 1973 National Association for the Advancement of Coloured People.

Molly Peacock, 'Mental France', copyright © Mollie Peacock 1984.

Alejandra Pizarnik, 'Sigus', copyright © this translation Susan Bassnett 1990.

'The Zoo Keeper's Wife' from *The Collected Poems* by Sylvia Plath, published by Faber & Faber Ltd, copyright © Ted Hughes 1971 and 1981, by permission of Olwyn Hughes, and *The Collected Poems of Sylvia Plath*, edited by Ted Hughes, copyright © 1960, 1965, 1971, 1981 by the estate of Sylvia Plath, by permission of Harper & Row, Publishers Inc.

Marsha Prescod, 'Vicious circle'; 'Love story? (part 2)', from *Land of Rope and Tory*, copyright © Marsha Prescod 1990.

Willis Barnstone, translator, for Princess Zeb-un-Nissa, 'Though I am Laila of the Persian romance', from *A Book of Women Poets*, Schocken Books, reprinted by permission copyright © these translations Willis Barnstone 1980.

Deborah Randall, – 'Ballygrand widow', from *The Sin Eater*, Bloodaxe Books Ltd, 1989, reprinted by permission Bloodaxe Books Ltd, and copyright © Deborah Randell 1989.

Carlyle Reedy, from 'The kiss', copyright © Carlyle Reedy 1967, 1990.

Adrienne Rich, from 'Twenty-one love poems', II, III, from *The Dream of a Common Language, Poems 1974–77*, reprinted by permission of W.W. Norton & Company, Inc., copyright © 1978 by W.W. Norton & Company Inc.

Denise Riley, 'Affections must not', from *Dry Air*, Virago Press, 1985, originally published *Marxism for Infants*, Street Editions, Cambridge, 1977. Reprinted by permission and copyright © Denise Riley 1977, 1985.

Michèle Roberts, – 'Magnificat', from *Mirror of The Mother*, Methuen London, reprinted by permission Methuen London and copyright © Michèle Roberts 1986.

Muriel Rukeyser, 'Looking at each other', from *The Collected Poems of Muriel Rukeyser*,

Maura Stanton, 'Visibility', from *Cries of Swimmers*, University of Utah Press 1984. Reprinted by permission and copyright © Maura Stanton 1984.

Gertrude Stein, 'A Sonatina Followed by Another' – extract, from *Bee Time Vine and Other Pieces*, 1913–27, Vol. 3 of the Unpublished Works of Gertrude Stein, reprinted by kind permission Yale University Press, copyright © the executors of the Estate of Alice B. Toklas 1953.

Anne Stevenson, 'The Victory', 'Himalayan Balsam', from *Selected Poems 1956–1986*, reprinted by kind permission Oxford University Press and author, copyright © Anne Stevenson, 1987.

Alfonsina Storni, 'Little-bitty man', from *Selected Poems*, ed. Marion Freeman, White Pine Press, reprinted by permission. copyright © this translation Marion Freeman 1957.

Rita Anyiam St John, 'For me from you', from *Watchers & Seekers*, eds Cobham R, & Collins, M, The Women's Press, 1987, reprinted by permission of the author, copyright © Rita Anyiam St. John 1987.

Janet Sutherland, 'To the spider in the crevice', from *Dancing the Tightrope: New Love Poems by Women*, Women's Press, 1987, reprinted by permission and copyright © Janet Sutherland 1987.

May Swenson, 'Little lion face', from *In Other Words*, Reprinted by permission Alfred A. Knopf, Inc., copyright © May Swenson 1987.

Sylvia Townsend Warner, 'Drawing you heavy with sleep'; 'Under the sudden blue', from *Collected Poems*, reprinted by permission Carcanet Press Ltd, copyright © the executors of the Estate of Sylvia Townsend Warner 1982.

Marina Tsvetaeva, 'Where does this tenderness come from'; 'You loved me'; from 'Poem of the End' (Section 5), from *Selected Poems* Oxford University Press, reprinted by kind permission Olwyn Hughes, copyright © this translation Elaine Feinstein 1981.

Nika Turbina, 'The return', from *First Draft*, reprinted by kind permission, Marion & Boyars, London & New York, this translation by Elaine Feinstein and Antonina Bouis, copyright © Marion Boyars Publications 1988.

Chase Twichell, 'Physics', from *Northern Spy*, University of Pittsburgh Press, 1981, reprinted by permission of the publisher and copyright © P. Chase Twichell 1981.

Doina Uricariu, 'Small splinters from my cheek', from *Silent Voices: An Anthology of Romanian Women Poets*, Forest Books, reprinted by permission publishers & translator, copyright © this translation Brenda Walker and Andrea Deletant 1986.

Shadab Vajdi, 'Illiterate', from *Closed Circuit*, Forest Books, translated by Lotfali Khaji, reprinted by permission publisher and poet, copyright © Shadab Vajdi 1989.

Patrizia Vicinelli, 'Jade, or the Medea within us', published by permission poet and translators, copyright © this translation Tom Raworth & Franco Beltrametti 1989.

Gill Vickers, 'sun', from *An Untitled First Collection of Poems*, R. Books, Cambridge and Cheltenham, 1969, copyright © Gill Vickers 1969.

Solveig von Schoultz, 'The Lover'; 'The Rain' from *Snow and Summers*, Forest Books,

Index of Poets

Index of First Lines

THE COMPLETE COLLECTED POEMS OF MAYA ANGELOU

Maya Angelou

'You will hear the regal women; the mischievous street girl . . . Black, bitter and beautiful, she speaks of our survival' – *James Baldwin*

'Maya Angelou writes from the heart and her language rings clear and true . . . whether joyful or playful, her poems speak with delicacy and depth of feeling' – *M.F.K. Fisher*

Published for the first time in one exuberant volume, Maya Angelou's poetry is just as much a part of her life as her famous autobiography. With lyrical and dramatic skill, she winds skeins of longing and desire, throws punches – tough and tender – as she writes about freedom and shattered dreams. Her profound and inspiring poem, 'On the Pulse of Morning', written for President Clinton's inauguration, is also included. History in the making, heartbreak and freedom – these are Maya Angelou's themes so richly explored in cadences and rhythms of infinite inventiveness.

MORNING IN THE BURNED HOUSE

Margaret Atwood

'A novelist and poet of great gifts' – *Guardian*

'Margaret Atwood is the quiet Mata Hari, the mysterious, violent figure . . . who pits herself against the ordered, too-clean world like an arsonist' – *Michael Ondaatje*

By turns dark, playful, intensely moving, tender and intimate – these poems are Atwood's most accomplished, mature and versatile, *'setting foot on the middle ground/ between body and world.'* Here is that wickedly dry, humorous voice – Helen of Troy appears as a tabletop dancer, Miss July muses on life as a cheesecake queen and Cressida reveals what she really thought of Troilus. And here too are personal poems that concern themselves with love, with memory, with the fragility of the natural world. A beautiful elegiac series of meditations on the death of a parent, completes this generous and disturbing collection of wonderful, rare poems.

ROTTEN POMERACK

Merle Collins

'*Rotten Pomerack* is the witty, passionate, long-memoried verse testament of a singularly challenging, incorruptible and resonant Grenadian story-teller.' – *Michael Horovitz*

At the heart of this fiercely haunting volume of poems is an ardent spirit of storytelling. Voices whisper or shout or quietly call attention to some particular experience, whether personal or political – the longing for 'home' wherever it may be and the balm of forgetting. For the women and men in these poems, their stories begin in the Caribbean and move to England ('*nearly ten years later/look me here analysing/still distraught and debating/ sympathising synthesising/regretting and remembering/and time just passing*'). These poems are about the ironies and paradoxes of living – the proverbial slipping on a 'rotten pomerack' (French-Creole for the cashew fruit) which can make events take an unexpected turn – but most of all they are poems that break the listening silence.

THE VIRAGO BOOK OF WICKED VERSE

Edited by Jill Dawson

This wonderfully sharp and witty collection of poems – feisty, bawdy, erotic, irreverent – is an illuminating comment on women's ability to transform poetry into a medium of subversiveness. There are jibes at hypocrisy and prejudice, plenty of sexiness and sauciness, and a riotous turning of the 'Lady Poet' image on its head ('A falling leaf could stir her./A wilting, dying rose/would make her write, both day and night,/the most rewarding prose./She's find a hidden meaning/in every pair of pants/then hurry home to be alone/and write about romance' – *Maya Angelou*). With poets spanning continents and centuries, this anthology demonstrates lavishly the myriad ways in which women can be 'wicked' – by their definition – and wilfully so!

Poems by: Aphra Behn, Nina Cassian, Wendy Cope, Eunice de Souza, Emily Dickinson, Carol Ann Duffy, Lorna Goodison, Jackie Kay, Liz Lochhead, Suniti Namjoshi, Grace Nichols, Fiona Pitt-Kethley, Vicki Raymond, Ntozake Shange, Izumi Shikibu, Anna Wickham and many more.

THE VIRAGO BOOK OF LOVE & LOSS

Edited by Georgina Hammick

'Wonderful' – Wendy Cope, *Daily Telegraph*

'A glittering array of stories . . . all is various, all is luminous' – Elspeth Barker, *Independent on Sunday*

Elizabeth Bowen, Janette Turner Hospital, Doris Lessing, Shena Mackay, Alice Munro, Grace Paley, Dorothy Parker and Sylvia Townsend Warner are among the writers whose considerable talents feature in this memorable exploration of love and loss.

Here is the subterfuge and yearning of an illicit relationship, the intolerable oppression of summer in the face of a loved one's death and a mother who obscures her loneliness with irascible complaints to her son. Alongside stories of love's frailties are those shadowed by lost opportunities, lingering regrets and the bruising of age. This seductive collection brings together some of the foremost women writers of this century. Whether devastating or poignant, or glistening with wry humour, these stories reach into the corners of the heart.

THE SELECTED POEMS OF ANNE SEXTON

Edited by Diane Wood Middlebrook and
Diana Hume George

Anne Sexton could be called the first poet of
contemporary women. She spoke of her life as no
woman before her had dared to speak.

Her language was simple, domestic; her imagery
arresting; her subject matter urgent, shocking and
exciting. She wrote about mental breakdown, sex,
addiction, abortion – the other side of ordinary life.
Only four years after she began writing, Anne Sexton
published *To Bedlam and Part Way Back*, and went on to
win the 1967 Pulitzer Prize with her third book, *Live or
Die*. Top fees for her readings were hers for the asking;
her friends included Maxine Kumin, Robert Lowell and
Sylvia Plath. But fame could not cure her 'madness' and
in October 1974, aged 45, she committed suicide. Edited
and with an introduction by Diane Wood Middlebrook
(author of *Anne Sexton: A Biography*, Virago) and Diana
Hume George, this selection celebrates one of America's
most widely-read poets, at the height of her remarkable
powers.

SUNRIS

Grace Nichols

In this, her fourth and long-awaited collection, Grace Nichols celebrates roots and the flight from roots in sensuous soaring imagery. Her impressive long poem 'Sunris' is arguably the most sustained and original work on carnival in the female voice. Inspired by the infectious rhythms and bravado of carnival, 'Sunris' sweeps up the reader into the crowd whose journey moves to calypso's hypnotic pulse. In other poems, Grace Nichols visits the wet green hills of Windover England, where the Long-Man lies, and sends a letter as the Queen of Sheba. Spanning continents and histories, legend and ritual, this is a memorable collection from one of Britain's best loved Caribbean poets.

THE VIRAGO BOOK OF WOMEN'S WAR POETRY AND VERSE

Edited by Catherine Reilly

An omnibus edition of **Scars Upon my Heart** and **Chaos of the Night**

The voices of Sassoon and Owen on the male agony of the trenches are familiar ones, but less commonly heard is what the wartime years meant for millions of British women – both at home, as evacuees or as nurses in the trenches abroad. This impressive, moving anthology records women's experience of war – the hope for peace and reunion as well as the devastating upheavals and terrible loss suffered.

Includes poetry by Phyllis Shand Allfrey, Vera Brittain, Joyce Grenfell, Rose Macaulay, Charlotte Mew, Naomi Mitchinson, May Sinclair, Edith Sitwell, Stevie Smith, Marie Stopes, Sylvia Townsend Warner.

ALL THE SELVES I WAS

Michèle Roberts

'Michèle Roberts plays with duplicitous language, uncovering possibilities hidden in even the most mystifying metaphors' – *Times Literary Supplement*

'A strongly visual writer . . . Roberts can summon a landscape or domestic interior in a few vivid strokes and splashes of primary colour' – *Carol Rumens*

Michèle Roberts has written and published her poetry to high acclaim throughout her literary career. Her poems, rich in allusion – biblical and mythological – examine her continuing preoccupations with love, death, food and sex, working through metaphor to create a way of looking at the world which links the body/self to others, to nature, to life in the city. As she excavates from memory meanings that lie beneath the surface of ordinary life, she dissolves boundaries with sensuous and passionate clarity.

Now you can order superb titles directly from Virago

☐	The Complete Collected Poems	Maya Angelou	£9.99
☐	Morning in the Burned House	Margaret Atwood	£8.99
☐	Rotten Pomerack	Merle Collins	£8.99
☐	The Virago Book of Wicked Verse	Jill Dawson (ed)	£8.99
☐	The Virago Book of Love & Loss	Georgina Hammick (ed)	£6.99
☐	The Selected Poems of Anne Sexton	Diane Wood Middlebrook and Diana Hume George	£8.99
☐	Sunris	Grace Nichols	£7.99
☐	The Virago Book of Women's War Poetry and Verse	Catherine Reilly (ed)	£10.99
☐	All the Selves I Was	Michèle Roberts	£8.99
☐	The Haunting of Sylvia Plath	Jacqueline Rose	£8.99

Please allow for postage and packing: **Free UK delivery**.
Europe; add 25% of retail price; Rest of World; 45% of retail price.

To order any of the above or any other Virago titles, please call our
credit card orderline or fill in this coupon and send/fax it to:

Virago, 250 Western Avenue, London, W3 6XZ, UK.
Fax 0181 324 5678   Telephone 0181 324 5516

☐ I enclose a UK bank cheque made payable to Virago for £.............
☐ Please charge £.............. to my Access, Visa, Delta, Switch Card No.

☐☐☐☐☐☐☐☐☐☐☐☐☐☐☐☐☐☐☐

Expiry Date ☐☐☐☐   Switch Issue No.   ☐☐

NAME (Block letters please) ....

ADDRESS ....

....

....

Postcode ....Telephone ....

Signature ....

Please allow 28 days for delivery within the UK. Offer subject to price and availability.

Please do not send any further mailings from companies carefully selected by Virago ☐